I0797748

Question, connect and take action to become better citizens with a brighter future. Now that's smart thinking!

BUILDING HOMES FOR ALL

TECHNOLOGY FOR A FAIR AND GREEN PLANET

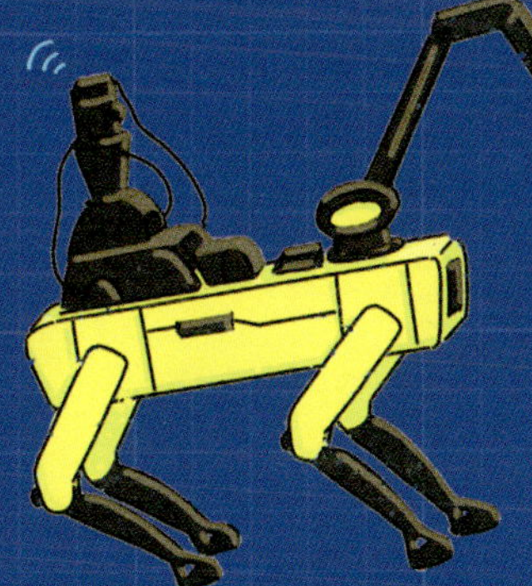

ELAINE KACHALA

ILLUSTRATED BY

CATHERINE CHAN

ORCA BOOK PUBLISHERS

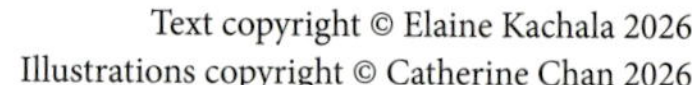

Text copyright © Elaine Kachala 2026
Illustrations copyright © Catherine Chan 2026

Published in Canada and the United States in 2026 by Orca Book Publishers.

All rights are reserved, including those for text and data mining, artificial intelligence (AI) training and similar technologies. No part of this publication may be reproduced or transmitted in any form or by any means, electronic or mechanical, including photocopying, recording or by any information storage and retrieval system now known or to be invented, without permission in writing from the publisher. The publisher expressly prohibits the use of this work in connection with the development of any software program, including, without limitation, training a machine-learning or generative AI system.

Library and Archives Canada Cataloguing in Publication
Title: Building homes for all : technology for a fair and green planet / Elaine Kachala ; illustrated by Catherine Chan.
Names: Kachala, Elaine, author | Chan, Catherine (Illustrator), illustrator.
Series: Orca think ; 21.
Description: Series statement: Orca think ; 21 | Includes bibliographical references and index.
Identifiers: Canadiana (print) 20250161990 | Canadiana (ebook) 20250163411 | ISBN 9781459839564 (hardcover) | ISBN 9781459839588 (EPUB) | ISBN 9781459839571 (PDF)
Subjects: LCSH: Ecological houses—Technological innovations—Juvenile literature. | LCSH: House construction—Environmental aspects—Juvenile literature. | LCSH: Dwellings—Technological innovations—Juvenile literature. | LCSH: Dwellings—Design and construction—Juvenile literature. | LCSH: Housing—Juvenile literature.
Classification: LCC TH4860 .K33 2026 | DDC j728/.047—dc23

Library of Congress Control Number: 2025934599

Summary: Part of the nonfiction Orca Think series for middle-grade readers, this illustrated book introduces young readers to innovative building techniques that will make homes sustainable and accessible to everyone.

Orca Book Publishers is committed to reducing the consumption of nonrenewable resources in the production of our books. We make every effort to use materials that support a sustainable future.

Orca Book Publishers gratefully acknowledges the support for its publishing programs provided by the following agencies: the Government of Canada, the Canada Council for the Arts and the Province of British Columbia through the BC Arts Council and the Book Publishing Tax Credit.

The author and publisher have made every effort to ensure that the information in this book was correct at the time of publication. The author and publisher do not assume any liability for any loss, damage, or disruption caused by errors or omissions. Every effort has been made to trace copyright holders and to obtain their permission for the use of copyrighted material. The publisher apologizes for any errors or omissions and would be grateful if notified of any corrections that should be incorporated in future reprints or editions of this book.

The author wishes to thank the Ontario Arts Council and the Government of Ontario for their support.

Design by Troy Cunningham.
Edited by Kirstie Hudson.

Printed and bound in South Korea.

29 28 27 26 • 1 2 3 4

CERTIFIED CANADIAN PUBLISHER

ORCA BOOK PUBLISHERS
orcabook.com

For my family.
Thank you for making our house
our home.

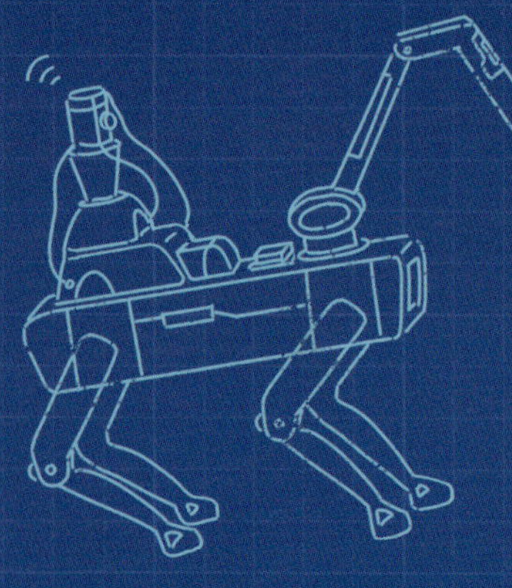

CONTENTS

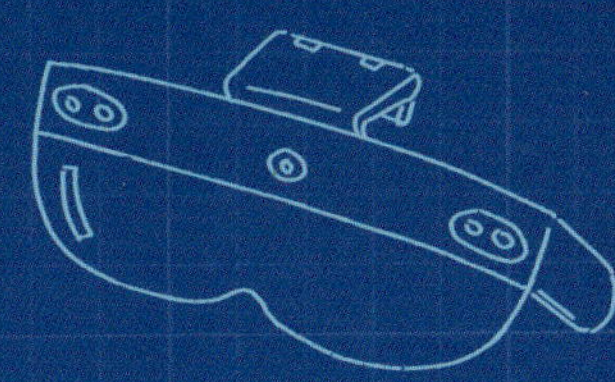

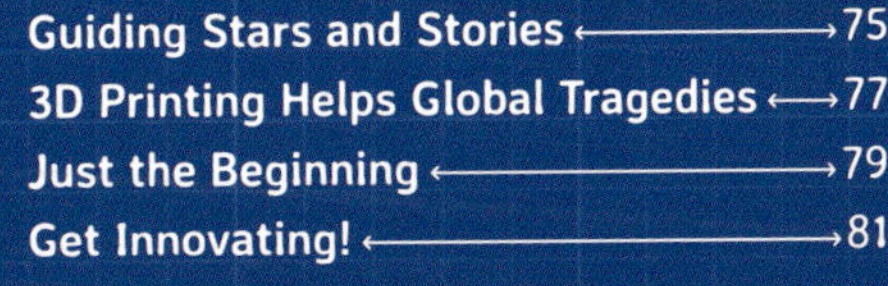

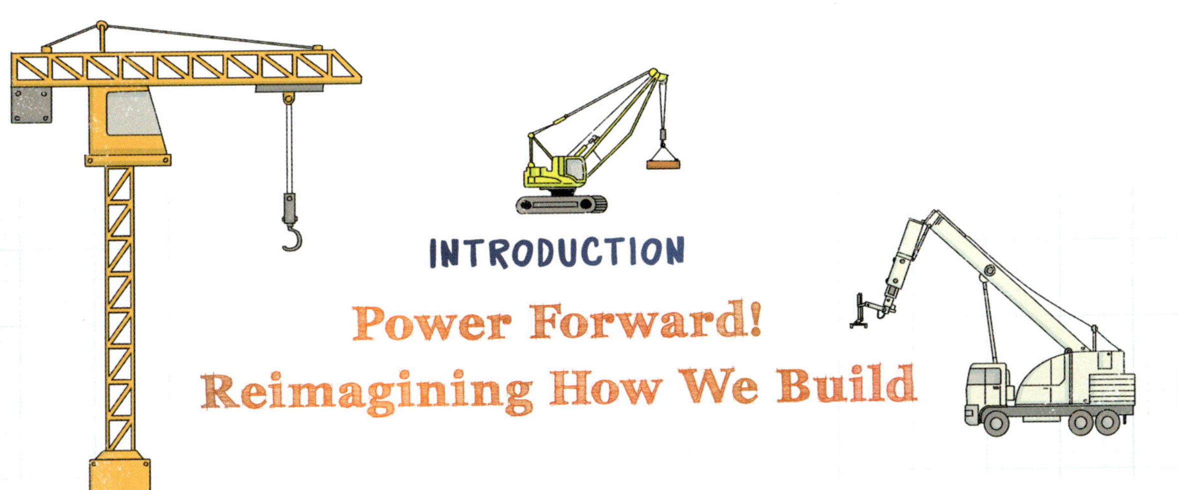

INTRODUCTION

Power Forward! Reimagining How We Build

Guess how many humans there are in the world? There are over 8 billion of us scattered around the planet. Guess how many there will be by 2050? Almost 10 billion! People everywhere should have somewhere to live and call home. That means a safe, healthy, affordable place that meets their needs.

But there's a problem. In almost every country, people are struggling to find and pay for housing. In cities and towns, everyone's talking about how buying or renting a place is too expensive for hard-working people. You might have heard one of these stories. Maybe you know someone who told you they can't find an affordable place to live. Perhaps you or your family struggles to find a place to call home.

"We are off track!" reported the United Nations. The global building and construction sector won't achieve decarbonization by 2050. We must use innovative technologies and sustainable building materials to help get on track.
CHUNYIP WONG/GETTY IMAGES

The United Nations Human Settlements Program (UN-Habitat) estimates that 96,000 new affordable homes need to be built every day until 2030 to meet our housing needs. The world needs more homes, built faster. But here's the thing—building homes for 10 billion people pollutes the environment. In fact, buildings and construction are

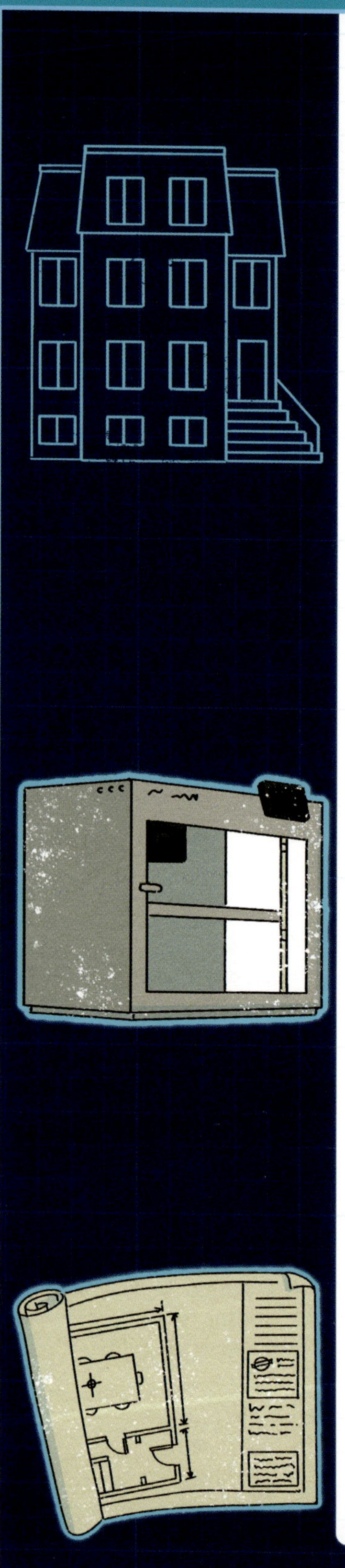

responsible for more than 40 percent of the world's ***carbon dioxide (CO_2)*** emissions. The production and use of concrete, steel, glass and bricks unleash tons of greenhouse gases.

The world is facing a double whammy—a housing shortage *and* a climate crisis. We need more houses built faster *without* polluting the earth. Is your brain starting to hurt? You're not alone. But wait!

Clean, Green, Smart Construction

What if you could push a button and a machine would 3D-print eco-friendly houses in months, weeks or even days? What if you could 3D-print them from low CO_2 concrete, raw earth, wood fiber or plastic, and ***upcycle*** and recycle the tons of waste that are dumped in our rivers, lakes and seas? What if you could quickly manufacture modular, mass-timber buildings in state-of-the-art factories? And what if these wood buildings could slow climate change? What if robots, drones, ***wearable devices*** and immersive technologies were our superhelpers? And why stop at Earth? NASA is working with companies to build 3D-printed shelters for missions to the moon and Mars. What they're learning is helping construction technology for homes here on Earth.

These ideas might seem far-fetched and futuristic, but they're happening. The future of construction is here. Creative thinkers and leaders around the world are reimagining ways to build, from start to finish.

Hello, Technology! Meet Collaboration

Can technology improve how we build housing? Absolutely! For decades people have been struggling to fix the housing

CONSTRUCTION SITE of the FUTURE

The construction industry is one of the most important industries in the world. But it's been *way* behind other industries when it comes to using new technologies—until now. The world is at a turning point in construction ***automation***.

crisis. They've been running out of ideas. With the advent of new technologies, however, they're inspired.

But can technology alone get us out of this double-whammy crisis? No way! Something else is needed—collaboration! It takes teamwork to challenge rules and old ways of doing things.

Construction Zone—Please Enter!

In this book you'll meet trailblazers who are proving that construction can be done differently to build faster, better, safer, cheaper and greener. You'll discover how engineers, architects, builders, business leaders and government officials are working together and harnessing the power of innovative technologies. Is innovation risky? Is it scary? You bet! It takes learning, experimenting, making mistakes and spending time and money. It takes guts! But *not* innovating is way riskier. The world's housing and climate crises need solutions—*now*!

Help wanted! The construction world needs new minds, including yours. Let's imagine how we can build better homes for everyone.

ONE

What Does Home Mean?

Have you ever thought about what having a home means? A place of one's own has special meaning for each of us.

Habitat for Humanity Canada is part of a global nonprofit housing organization. It works with communities, businesses and governments to build families safe, decent, affordable homes. Every year it runs a contest called Meaning of Home, asking kids to submit a poem or short story about what having a home means to them. The prize money goes to the winner's local Habitat for Humanity to build a home in their community.

Cooking together at home makes mealtimes a fun tradition. Families prepare delicious food, make precious memories and learn healthy eating habits.

HALFPOINT IMAGES/GETTY IMAGES

The Many Meanings of Home

A home isn't just a place to live. The students' poems and stories express how they see their home as a haven of love, joy, comfort, safety and so much more. That's because home is at the root of our well-being.

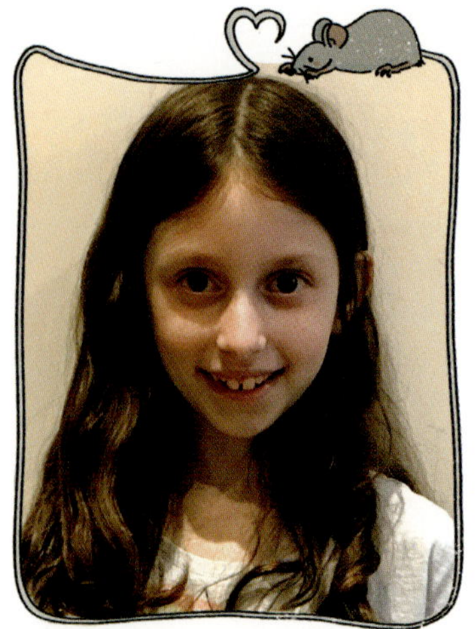

DAPHNE USTER

"NO PLACE LIKE HOME"

BY DAPHNE

Home is a place with family and friends.
It has a chain of love that never ends...
Habitat for Humanity builds houses
for people without a home.
It might even have a garden gnome!
I try to help my community too.
Everyone can, including you!...

KRISTY LEROUX

"HOME SWEET HOME"

BY PEYTON

Home. The place where I can cuddle
up for a family movie night.
The popping sound of fresh popcorn and
the buttery smell filling the air.
The smiles on our faces as we laugh together.
The taste of a homemade ice cream sundae on my lips.
I'm comfortable, safe and warm. I feel loved.
Home. The neighborhood where I have grown up...

SASKIA VAN DER SPUY

"IF HOME WERE THE 5 SENSES"

BY RYLAN

If home were a sight, it would be the most
beautiful pink sunset you have ever seen.
If home were a sound, it would be the laughter of
my family around the kitchen table at dinner
time and hearing my grandparents say, "I love you."...
Everyone deserves to have their own space where
they feel safe and protected; a place that is warm
and cozy and a shelter from rain and snow...

Swimming Upstream

Habitat for Humanity says that having a home equals health, safety, security and an opportunity for a better future, and that clean, well-built, affordable housing also unlocks our human potential. They're right! For over 150 years scientists have been saying that our housing conditions affect our physical, mental and social health. Imagine trying to swim upstream against a raging current. It would be tough. The current would constantly push you back. Now imagine trying to live a healthy, happy, creative and successful life without a clean, safe home. Maybe you don't have to imagine because you're struggling with this very thing. It's hard—and unfair.

Where do you cook healthy meals or do homework? Where do you sleep without a place to put a comfy bed? What do you do if you don't have a quiet space for thinking, pursuing hobbies or hanging out with friends? How do you protect yourself from rain or snow? Not having a home would feel like swimming upstream against a raging current.

Over two million people volunteer with Habitat for Humanity worldwide. It's a fun and rewarding way to give back.
BURT JOHNSON/DREAMSTIME.COM

Big Forces

Our health and well-being are affected by the conditions we're born into and grow up in, and they're all connected. The World Health Organization calls these conditions the "social determinants of health." Having clean, safe housing in a secure neighborhood is one condition. Other conditions are having healthy food, clean air and drinking water, and enough income—and also the opportunity to go to a safe school and get a good education. Being employed and working in a secure environment are other conditions. People also need healthcare and social support from friends, family and the community. And they need to have positive early childhood experiences and be able to live free from racism and discrimination.

Having a quiet, safe space at home to do homework can help kids do better at school. After all, learning doesn't stop when school's out for the day.

ANDRESR/GETTY IMAGES

Just how much of a difference can bad housing make? Researchers say people, including kids, living in overcrowded or dirty conditions get sick more often and die younger than those living in clean, safe conditions. Poor housing affects mental health, as living in bad conditions or worrying about being thrown out of your house is stressful. It can cause anxiety or depression. Sometimes people choose unhealthy coping methods, like drugs, alcohol or smoking. Then guess what? These things make people sick too. Sadly, poor-quality housing can start a cycle of illness and death.

FINLAND TAKES ACTION

Give everyone a home! It may sound simple, but it takes work and a new way of thinking. Housing First is a program that began in North America in the 1990s and spread to other countries. Finland made a national plan with housing as its top priority. The government worked with cities and organizations and created tailor-made plans to help people fix the problems that led to their ***homelessness***. Finland proved it! If people have homes, it's easier for them to fix other issues like mental health issues or drug addictions. It's one of the only countries where rates of homelessness are decreasing. Finland plans to end homelessness by 2027.

Researchers have also established links between housing and opportunity. For example, they compared kids and youth who lived in safe, healthy homes with those who didn't. Those living in poor housing conditions did worse in school. They were also more likely to have injuries and accidents and become involved in crime.

AFFORDABLE HOUSING or HOUSING AFFORDABILITY?

Affordable housing is also called social housing or public housing. It's specially built housing that governments help pay for (subsidize) if people have low income or no income. Governments in Canada and the United States say housing is affordable when their citizens don't need to spend more than 30 percent of their paychecks to put a roof over their heads. Some say even 30 percent is too much. Shouldn't we all be able to afford housing and have money left for things like food, clothing, medicine and other necessities?

Housing Is a Human Right—Full Stop!

In 1948 the United Nations (UN) included the right to safe housing in its Universal Declaration of Human Rights. In 1966 it adopted two international agreements that are powerful statements of citizens' rights. UN member countries signed and agreed to follow those sets of rights. Sadly, even though member countries signed the agreements, not all recognize housing as a legal human right. Even if they do, they still have housing problems. Framing housing as a human right is an important first step. But it takes *way more* than a law for everyone to have safe, healthy housing that's affordable.

Building homes for everyone is a difficult problem. But when people and technologies work together, powerful changes are possible. We *can* fix one of the biggest forces affecting people's health and well-being.

In 2019 the Canadian government passed the National Housing Strategy Act. It includes the declaration that housing is a human right. Governments and organizations must have a plan for safe housing that meets citizens' needs.

PETER MARSHALL/
ALAMY STOCK PHOTO

TWO

Why Don't People Have Homes?

From east to west and north to south, millions of people worldwide need affordable homes. How did this crisis happen? Many complicated reasons have been piling up for years.

The main thing is that there simply aren't enough affordable homes for a growing population. Governments and builders have not been constructing homes fast enough, and the homes they are building don't meet the needs of different people—there's a shortage and a mismatch! The issues in this chapter explain *some* of the reasons why.

The built environment matters! It affects our health and the natural environment. Construction touches all aspects of our lives and boosts our economy. It's time to do better with innovation and new technologies.

IVARS KISIS/SHUTTERSTOCK.COM

Old Building Methods

We're still building like we did a hundred years ago. There are too many parts, materials and steps. It's hard to organize tradespeople with different skills and from many companies, and supplies are hard to get. Not only is construction slow, but it's also one of the biggest contributors to the world's climate crisis. CO_2 emissions come from sourcing and using concrete,

steel, glass and bricks. They come from manufacturing and construction methods and from the energy it takes to cool or heat buildings. Even demolition adds emissions. Construction also uses many of the world's resources, including water. It contributes to air and water pollution and landfill waste—*megatons* of waste. For all these reasons, construction is slow, wasteful, polluting, dangerous and expensive.

The numbers are alarming. In Canada, more than 20 percent of the construction labor force will retire in the next 10 years. Over 150,000 skilled workers are urgently needed. Solving the labor crisis requires all hands on deck and new solutions.

ARLAWKA AUNGTUN/ GETTY IMAGES

Labor Crunch

There aren't enough human hands to build the homes we need! The National Association of Home Builders in the United States says there is a major labor shortage—we need more skilled construction workers. The problem is worldwide. Older, experienced workers are retiring, and young people aren't choosing careers in construction. Governments and building associations are working to encourage young people to choose construction careers.

Not Embracing Technology

When it comes to automation, construction is behind other industries. The production of almost everything today is automated—our clothes, cars, appliances, you name it—but not housing! Why not? For one thing, innovation is risky. Governments make many rules to ensure that buildings are

Construction automation is the most important change for helping address the world's housing and climate crisis.

(MAIN) SUMMIT ART CREATIONS SHUTTERSTOCK.COM; (INSET) PANUPONG PIEWKLENG/ GETTY IMAGES

safe, and they're not quick to change them. Insurance companies are cautious too. They won't easily provide insurance for new materials or methods. Innovation is expensive, but banks aren't quick to lend money. It's also hard to convince investors to give big money. Plus it takes time for people to get comfortable with new technologies.

These reasons make sense, to a point. Everyone wants to live in safe buildings. But *never* adopting new materials and methods—that's extreme. Experts are ringing the alarm bells! We'll only create the affordable housing we need and address the climate problems the construction industry creates if we adopt new ways. We must learn to build differently.

Choosing to do something different isn't easy, but letting go of old habits and ideas can lead to exciting new opportunities.
SYHINSTAS/GETTY IMAGES

Old Ideas

Letting go of old ideas is hard. Humans don't like change! Still, old attitudes are barriers to innovation. "We're always chasing emergencies," says Dan Heath. He's a researcher and author of a book called *Upstream: The Quest to Solve Problems Before They Happen.* "We respond after the bad thing has happened. We don't go upstream to solve problems at their root." Why not?

It's because upstream thinking and prevention are harder to act on, says Heath. For example, solving complicated problems like homelessness is not one person's job. Governments and organizations must collaborate, but they're set up to work separately. People are assigned to solve different bits of problems. No one sees the whole picture or how issues start in the first place.

Also, prevention doesn't grab people's attention. It happens in the background, so it's hard to notice. But Heath says upstream thinking is powerful because solutions last over time. Finland is a great example. While the rest of the world is rushing to the homelessness scene with emergency services like shelters, governments and organizations in Finland are working together to provide permanent housing and social support.

People think prevention costs too much. Wrong! say researchers, and they've proved it. Building permanent homes might cost a lot, but in the end, preventing homelessness from happening in the first place saves society money.

Floods can damage or destroy homes, forcing people to find new places to live. People with low incomes are often unable to afford other places. With climate change, floods are getting worse and happening more often.
CID GUEDES/GETTY IMAGES

Believing Myths About Homelessness

Many situations can lead to homelessness—it's not just one thing. Understanding this fact is important, because believing myths gets in the way of preventing homelessness. The most common myths are that people choose to be homeless, homeless people are lazy or homeless people are all drug addicts. Myths and ***stereotypes*** like these ***stigmatize*** people experiencing homelessness and block society from understanding their challenges and finding solutions.

The fact is, researchers say, the cost of housing is the main reason why more people are becoming homeless. People can't afford places to live. The money people earn isn't keeping up with climbing housing costs. Along with the rising cost of food, medicine and clothes, people must make tough choices—eat or pay rent. Poverty causes homelessness.

Falling on Hard Times

There are other reasons people can become homeless. A company may go out of business, and people lose their jobs. Or people may lose their homes during war or natural disasters like fires or floods. Adults and kids who must flee violent home situations can end up homeless.

Injuries or illnesses can affect a person's ability to work and pay for a home. Veterans returning from war may suffer from mental health problems that prevent them from working, earning money and fitting back into civilian life. Sometimes mental health issues can cause homelessness. But they can also be the result of homelessness.

Everyone has a story. A person may experience a shocking situation that leads to drug addiction, which upsets their life, and they become homeless.

Some have friends and family that can offer a place to live, but others don't. Making sure people have a home is the human thing to do. Those who don't have homes are not bad, undeserving people—they're human beings without homes who are facing hard times. They deserve dignity, respect and help to turn their situations around.

Having to sleep in a tent on a freezing-cold winter day is tragic and not something anyone wants for their family. But sometimes it feels safer and more peaceful than being in a shelter crammed with other unhoused people.

DAVEMANTEL/GETTY IMAGES

Old Rules

Not only are we using old building methods, we're using old rules. Local governments like regions, cities or towns make zoning rules, which are laws that divide the land into zones (areas) and determine things like what types and sizes of buildings can be built or how much land is allowed for each building. For decades, zoning rules limited construction to single-family homes. They didn't allow different sizes of buildings and more affordable options such as stacked town-homes, attached homes and small apartments. These types of buildings, often called middle housing, have space for more people. Building them also reduces CO_2 emissions and makes better use of land, which is expensive and sometimes scarce. Today these outdated laws have prevented home building. Plus, by limiting the sizes and types of buildings, zoning creates pockets of wealthy areas and poor areas, and separates communities by race and class.

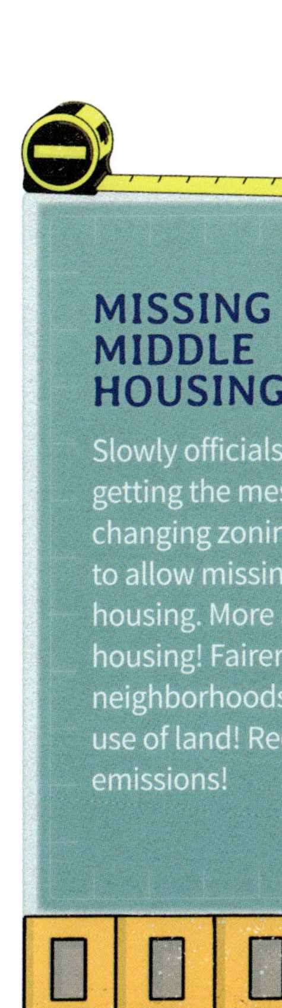

MISSING MIDDLE HOUSING

Slowly officials are getting the message and changing zoning laws to allow missing middle housing. More affordable housing! Fairer neighborhoods! Better use of land! Reduced CO_2 emissions!

Too Many Rules

Local governments also make building codes. The codes are strict rules about how tall buildings can be, what land can be used, what building materials are allowed and much more. Their purpose is to guide design and protect public health and safety and land. But sometimes they're so strict that they can stop building and innovation. Some people say too many rules mean we can't build on land we need for houses. But others wonder how we can balance the need for houses with protecting green space, farmland and wetland. Most people ask, How can we do both?

No One's In Charge

Countries usually have more than one level of government. For example, in Canada and the United States, powers are divided between federal, state or provincial, and local governments. Each one has a job to do when it comes to providing

housing for citizens. And each one has money and the power to make rules and laws. They share the responsibility for housing. The bad news is that this makes for a confusing situation, especially when they don't agree. The good news is that when they work with communities, solutions are possible.

Too expensive! Too small! Cities are filled with tall buildings full of expensive, tiny condominiums. Only the rich can afford them, and they don't have enough rooms for families. Governments and builders aren't building what most people need and can afford.
INSUNG JEON/GETTY IMAGES

Governments Dropped the Ball

Historically governments have allowed tall, expensive apartment buildings and condominiums and large houses to be built. Their ***policies*** haven't done enough to regulate and control some of the ***housing market*** so that people with different income levels, not just the rich, can afford a place. They also haven't made it easy, appealing or affordable for landowners, developers and builders to *want* to build different housing types. And, to top it off, governments haven't chipped in with enough money over the years to ensure that people with low incomes can afford homes.

SHOW ME the MONEY

Researchers say that when governments help people pay for a place to live and provide support, it can prevent homelessness. Professor Stephen Gaetz is president of the Canadian Observatory on Homelessness and the Homeless Hub. His motto is prevention, and his organization's Housing First for Youth model proves that it works. Gaetz says we prevent youth homelessness when they get safe housing and help with health, education, employment and fitting back into society. This reduces homelessness overall because youth are housed for good.

NIMBYism

Imagine your family wants to add more rooms to your house so your grandparents can move in. The law says that neighbors must be asked for approval. What if they say no because they don't like the design? There's a name for the neighbors' reaction. It's called NIMBYism—which means "not in my backyard!" Let's say elected officials agree with the neighbors. After all, the neighbors pay taxes and vote. NIMBYism is one of the main reasons that new or different types of housing, especially affordable housing, aren't built.

Experts say that consulting neighbors is important. We need to respect citizens' concerns, and often they have valid ones. But consulting should be limited to what the law requires and have a time limit. There must be a better balance between respecting citizens' opinions and building the housing people need.

More families are choosing to have multiple generations living together so they can share the high costs of housing.
SEWCREAMSTUDIO/GETTY IMAGES

No One Magic Nail!

There's no one magic nail to building homes for all. The world must tackle the housing crisis from many angles. That means shifting from

- downstream reacting *to* upstream preventing;
- thinking we can't solve the problem *to* a can-do attitude;
- building shelters *to* building permanent houses of all types and sizes;
- working separately *to* all governments working together with groups, companies, communities, builders, engineers, architects, business leaders and researchers;
- NIMBY *to* YIMBY (Yes in my backyard!);
- strict zoning laws *to* the right balance of rules that allow different types and sizes of buildings;
- letting people fend for themselves *to* governments chipping in—a lot;
- old building methods *to* adopting new technologies;
- and *way* more.

There's no time to waste! Read on to meet trailblazers who are reimagining the construction industry and exploring how technology can help.

THREE

Our Tech-Powered Partners

The world needs more homes built better, faster, more safely, more cheaply and greener. Technology can help! The construction industry has been slow to automate, but guess what? A revolution is happening. Robots are helping with tasks like bricklaying, digging, scanning, surveying, plastering, painting and rubble rooting. But the bots aren't doing it all! A lot of smart power is revolutionizing the construction industry, including virtual reality (VR), mixed reality (MR), augmented reality (AR) and exoskeletons, among others. Cutting-edge technologies are our helpers.

Immersive reality technologies like VR, MR and AR help at all stages of construction. Teams can work collaboratively with 3D models to improve planning, safety training, designing and building.

AKACIN PHONSAWAT/ GETTY IMAGES

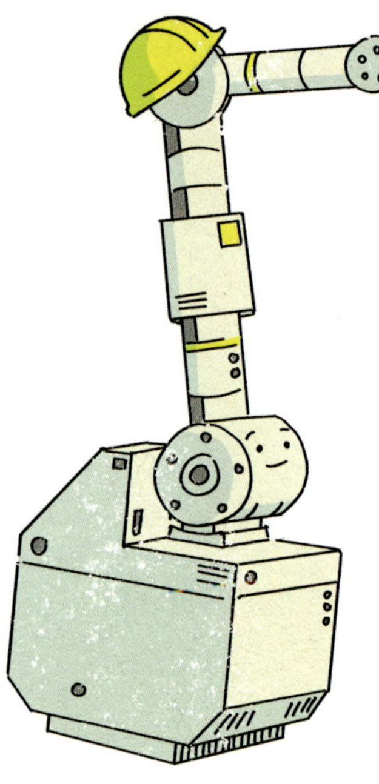

Construction Robots—Now Hiring!

Bots are great partners. They work faster, more accurately and for longer days than people do. Plus, they're perfect for the dull, dirty, difficult or dangerous jobs that people don't want to do. Humans can be the supervisors, and bots can help with the physically tough jobs!

But first, what is a robot? Whatever you're thinking, you're probably right. Robots are a diverse bunch. They differ hugely in size, shape, design and what they can do, so it's not easy to define them. Even robot experts have different ideas about what a robot is or isn't. But here's a definition that many can agree with: A robot is an ***autonomous*** machine. It can sense its environment, perform computations and decide on an action, and carry out that action in the real world. Sense, compute, act equals intelligence! A robot is constantly repeating this sensing-computing-acting cycle. Experts call it a feedback loop. It's this feedback loop that makes machines smart.

SENSE

Robots use different types of ***sensors***, such as laser, ***lidar*** and cameras, to detect information about their surroundings.

COMPUTE

Machine learning algorithms allow robots to "think." This means robots can process and understand information, solve problems, make decisions and perform tasks.

ACT

Some robots can move around, while others can manipulate things. Many can do both. Some can do specific tasks; others can do many things. Some are controlled remotely by human operators. Others run autonomously. Many rely on both. To act, a robot needs ***actuators.*** They're types of motors that push, pull or rotate and turn signal inputs into motion.

Brick- and Block-Layers

People can lay about 300 to 500 bricks a day. The next-generation Hadrian X can lay up to 500 FBR blocks (or about 2,500 standard bricks) per hour.

2025 FBR LIMITED

Meet Hadrian X—the world's first mobile, block-laying robot! FBR (once called Fastbrick Robotics) is the brains behind this smart machine. Hadrian X can lay regular bricks, but FBR is on an environmental mission. So they've made special blocks that are lighter, stronger, larger and more ***sustainable***.

Hadrian X is building townhomes and single-family homes in neighborhoods around Australia and the United States, and it will soon start in Europe. Hadrian X can build a single-story house in a day! It can also build houses of up to four stories. FBR uses a special construction glue that sticks the blocks together faster and stronger than mortar. "Bricklayers of the future will use Hadrian X as a tool," says FDR creator Mark Pivac. It does heavy, repetitive tasks and improves working conditions so that bricklayers can have longer, safer careers. Humans are still involved in the operation. They oversee the building plans, and a crew of two or three people operate Hadrian X from a tablet and supervise while the bot follows a 3D ***computer-aided design*** (***CAD***) model. It knows how many blocks it will use, and it can cut blocks to different sizes for later use. These functions reduce waste. Since there's no over-ordering or waste removal, money is saved too.

The next-generation Hadrian X has a 105-foot (32-meter) robotic arm with a claw at the end guided by motion sensors. It can adjust its position 1,000 times a second. Hadrian X also has advanced algorithms that track things like wind and vibration so it can steady itself and work accurately even when outdoor conditions change.

Noah Ready-Campbell is the founder and CEO of Built Robotics. Campbell grew up helping his carpenter dad build homes. It was hot, hard work. He later studied engineering and founded Built Robotics to create tools to help people build more efficiently.
BUILT ROBOTICS

Digging Deep

The Exosystem by Built Robotics is a robotic upgrade that turns an 80,000-pound (36,287-kilogram) excavator into a fully autonomous digger. Does a robot of that size scare you? It shouldn't! The company developed an eight-layer safety system with technologies such as ***radar***, ***GPS*** and AI-powered smart cameras for 360-degree vision. These technologies allow the robot to react automatically in less than a second. If it detects obstacles like people or vehicles, it stops until it's safe to start again. If operators want to control the Exosystem manually, they can at any time from a computer. The Exosystem is building new housing developments, solar farms, gas pipelines and other structures worldwide. With a command center in the ***cloud***, called Everest, workers can monitor, manage and operate it from anywhere in the world.

Scanning for Safety

Meet Spot, a four-legged robotic dog designed by engineers at Boston Dynamics. This bot is built to tackle tough tasks in many industries, including construction. Spot navigates rocky land, slippery steel beams, steep staircases and dark, dangerous, tight spaces such as tunnels with loose electrical wires or hazardous gases.

Spot takes commands from a human operator (using a tablet). It learns where to go and when to complete autonomous missions. With sensors, cameras, motors and software, Spot sees the world in 3D, maps its surroundings and does inspections. It also communicates in real time with a human team. Engineers test Spot's safety and reliability under the harshest conditions. For example, they put Spot in an oven, and they sent it through outdoor obstacle courses in wicked winters.

Spot doesn't spend all day wandering the streets. It does important work. The engineers at Boston Dynamics say Spot is a teammate and tool that helps workers build more safely.

NEWS ORESUND/WIKIMEDIA COMMONS/CC BY-SA 2.0

A company in London, England, called Foster + Partners was the first to use Spot to build apartments and homes, among other projects. On Spot's first day, someone ran to hug it! But this bot is more than just fun. "Spot's scans help us track projects to catch problems and ensure things are on time and conditions are safe," says Martha Tsigkari, one of the company's partners.

Surveying Sites

Is it a bird? Is it a plane? No. It's a drone! Drones are a type of robot. They can survey the land from various angles and provide vital information for home building because they're equipped with technologies such as lidar, sensors, cameras, GPS and machine-learning software. Drones can map property boundaries, examine building quality and

identify problems and solutions. Since there are many trades involved in building homes, such as architects, engineers and construction managers, drone ***data*** helps everyone track progress, materials and equipment. With "eyes" everywhere, drones can even catch theft on the job site. Drones save time and money and reduce the risk of injuries to humans working on construction sites.

Painting and Plastering Wizards

Okibo can paint an entire room (four walls) autonomously without stopping. This battery-operated bot can not only paint walls but also apply drywall, all the while scanning the area to ensure accuracy. Okibo operates alongside workers. But the workers don't need robotics training or knowledge of plastering and painting. Their job is to supervise, provide materials, make sure the battery is charged, take obstacles out of the robot's way and clean the airless spray machine at the end of the day.

Okibo can't cook your breakfast, but it sure can paint your house!
OKIBO

Rubble Rooters

Constructing and demolishing buildings produces megatons of waste—wood, wires, metal scraps, concrete, plastics and bricks. Usually it all ends up in landfills. Sorting these materials for recycling is hard and boring. It's dangerous, too, if the garbage contains sharp or contaminated objects. No one wants that job. Using robots to sort rubble and waste is a new industry. At Waste Robotics, bots are trained to learn to recognize, sort and grab different objects. And they are equipped with specialized computer vision, sensors and precisely made grippers.

It's already hard to find construction workers to build, and sorting waste is the last job people want, says Katherine Diamond, the marketing director at Waste Robotics. But for the sake of climate change and pollution, it's an important job.
ROMAN NOVITSKII/GETTY IMAGES

Safety First

Robotics offers many benefits to humans and creates exciting jobs that attract young people to construction. Still, experts agree we need to be cautious. It's important to pick the right robot for the right task and ensure that we design the bots to work safely together with humans.

The Exoskeletons Are Coming!

What flashes into your mind when you hear the word *exoskeleton*? Maybe it's images from live-action movies like *Iron Man* or *Avatar*. But do the powered exoskeletons (or robots) we have in real life look like these sci-fi devices? Not exactly...at least, not yet.

BOOST AND ASSIST

Exoskeletons might not be movie stars, but they sure are superstars on the construction site. Pushing, pulling, lifting, loading, holding, reaching and throwing—repetitive movements like these cause injuries and exhaustion for human workers. Exoskeletons are wearable devices that boost and assist people's physical activity. They work with our bodies to prevent injury and help with heavy or repetitive tasks.

Exoskeletons—exos, for short—come in a variety of designs and sizes for the whole body, upper body and lower body. Some are made from hard, stiff materials. Others, called exosuits, are made from soft, flexible materials.

Experts classify exos into two main types, active and passive. Only active exos are robotic. They're powered devices that support the body with additional energy. Batteries or electricity power the sensors, motors and other parts. Passive exos don't have a power source—they're not robotic. Human movement powers the device through a spring-like system such as levers or bands. Lifting, bending or carrying can put extreme force on a person's spine, legs, hips or arms. Passive exos redirect and reduce forces to make the job easier. They counterbalance (or offset) forces to decrease strain.

STRAP ON SMART POWER

Active exos like Apogee and Cray X are a new generation of smart robotic wearables. They support the worker's lower back and legs and help with lifting, loading, carrying, walking and bending. Motors kick in to assist the worker's muscles. These exos also have an intelligent system. Sensors detect problems with how a worker moves. Specialized software collects and analyzes the sensor data. The exo sends alerts if there are risks, such as the worker lifting or twisting the wrong way, or if the worker needs a break from a repetitive task. Engineers at German Bionic, the company that makes the suits, say they can study the data from the exo to understand safety risks and improve working environments.

The Apogee exoskeleton is German Bionic's newer, more advanced version. It's lightweight and more comfortable for longer use. The company is winning awards for its innovative smart power wearable designs.
GERMAN BIONIC

THE POWER OF SCIENCE

HeroWear's Apex 2 is one of the world's most researched and tested exoskeletons. This lightweight passive exosuit is winning awards and improving thousands of workers' lives across many industries, including construction. It doesn't have batteries or motors. The magic is in the elastic bands, say its inventors. Karl Zelik and Matt Yandell are engineers and scientists. They're also two of the cofounders of HeroWear. They say the exosuit works by channeling forces that typically go through the low back through elastic bands instead. The bands act like an extra set of back muscles to reduce or soak up some of that strain and fatigue. This design gives workers more energy and lowers injury risks.

CAUTION! OVERLOADED HUMAN

Exos hold real promise, but you can't just load up a human with a device. When you put on an exo that applies force, it affects a person's body. The HeroWear inventors had to ask a

HeroWear's Apex 2 exosuit attaches at a person's shoulders and thighs and has assistive bands (artificial back muscles) in between. There are different sizes to fit men and women of all shapes. It's strong but also light, soft, flexible and breathable.

HEROWEAR, LLC

lot of questions (see sidebar). Finding the answers means lots of testing in the lab and in the real world with workers. Then experts make standards for safety, quality, comfort, performance and other measures. These standards help people know which exos are best for different jobs and industries.

HEROWEAR INVENTORS ASK QUESTIONS

WHERE ON THE BODY IS THE BEST PLACE TO ATTACH AN EXO?

HOW MUCH FORCE CAN IT APPLY BEFORE IT HURTS?

HOW DO COMFORT LEVELS DIFFER AMONG PEOPLE?

DO COMFORT LEVELS CHANGE OVER MINUTES, HOURS OR DAYS?

To answer these questions, the inventors at HeroWear say that first they test the exo in the lab, and then they test it with thousands of real users on the job

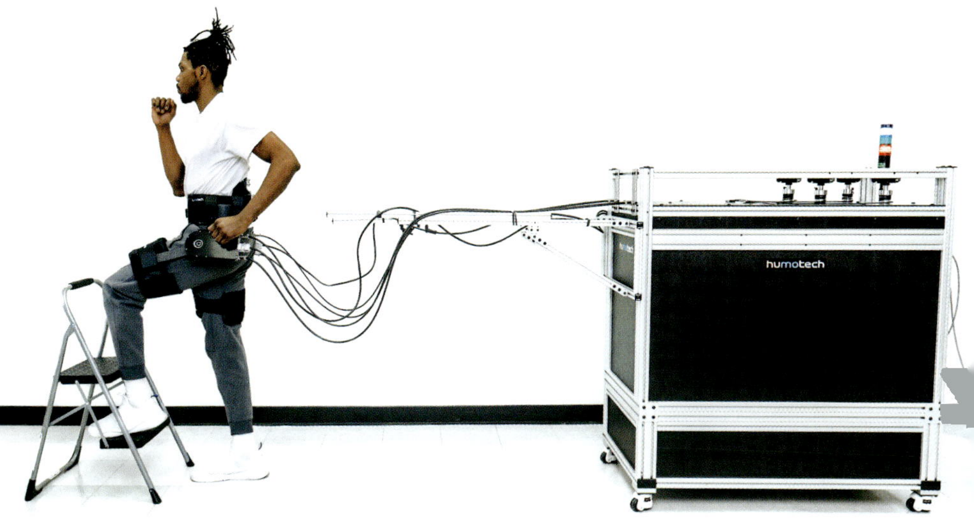

With the Caplex robotic system, scientists and engineers can apply different levels of force to the points where the wearable attaches to a person's body. Too much? Just right? Users told HeroWear exactly how much force assisted and felt comfortable.

LEE ANN STROMYER

First-Ever Wearable Development Tool

When inventors design wearables, there's a lot of testing, rebuilding and retesting, which takes time, money and parts. What if there were a robotic tool to do things better and faster? That was Josh Caputo's question. He put his science and engineering skills to work to find an answer. Caputo created the Caplex robotic system and a company called Humotech (short for Human Motion Technologies). It's groundbreaking, say researchers. The Caplex helps them design, test and build exoskeletons, prosthetics and other wearables. HeroWear's inventors used this system to perfect the Apex 2.

Know the Signs

Look out—human down! Wearables can also provide continuous safety monitoring and connection. For example, smart vests, shirts, boots, badges, clip-ons and watches have location and activity tracking. They can track vital signs like heart rate or body temperature. Some can detect falls or sense potential hazards, like dangerous heat or gases, and send emergency alerts.

Smart safety helmets have built-in technology such as AR, MR, sensors, internet and microphones. These helmets can help workers in many ways. For example, they can detect if the worker falls and send an emergency alert for help.

METAMORWORKS/GETTY IMAGES

Heating, ventilation and air-conditioning—check! With immersive technologies, teams can inspect entire construction designs and catch problems before building.

GORODENKOFF/GETTY IMAGES

Seeing Is Believing

What if you could plan and inspect a building's design before it's made? Or what if you could simulate dangers to train workers for safety? You can with immersive technologies. Augmented reality (AR), mixed reality (MR) and virtual reality (VR) help at different stages of construction.

With AR, you can overlay pictures, text, graphics, sounds and videos onto the real world. With a headset, smart glasses, phone or tablet, workers can see information such as how tall a building is or where pipes should go. Some AR gadgets can scan tags or labels. If you hover over them, text or 3D images pop up with alerts about possible hazards.

Like AR, MR adds digital information to the real world. But with MR you can move virtual objects around as if they were there. Usually workers wear a headset like Microsoft's HoloLens.

THAT'S NO GAME!

Feel what it's like to climb a 100-foot (30-meter) ladder. Know where to hook your harness or how far to stand from the roof's edge. VR training simulators help workers understand risks before going onto the construction site. They can learn how to manage heavy machinery or use their tools. Workers can get hands-on experience safely and prepare for real-life emergencies.

SOUTH_AGENCY/GETTY IMAGES

Full immersion! With VR you're no longer in the real world. By wearing a headset, you're totally immersed in a 360-degree, interactive, computer-generated world that you believe is real. You can teleport into a building that's being built, and it feels like you're there. Hand controllers allow you to interact with the digital environment. VR is the closest thing to a real construction-site experience.

Powerful Partners

People can use different technologies to improve the speed and safety of home building while doing a better job for less money. For example, CAD, AR, MR and VR can be used together with other tools like Building Information Modeling (BIM). It's a computer program that helps people work together to plan, design, build and run entire building projects in 3D. Using cloud computing, teams can work at the same time, no matter where each

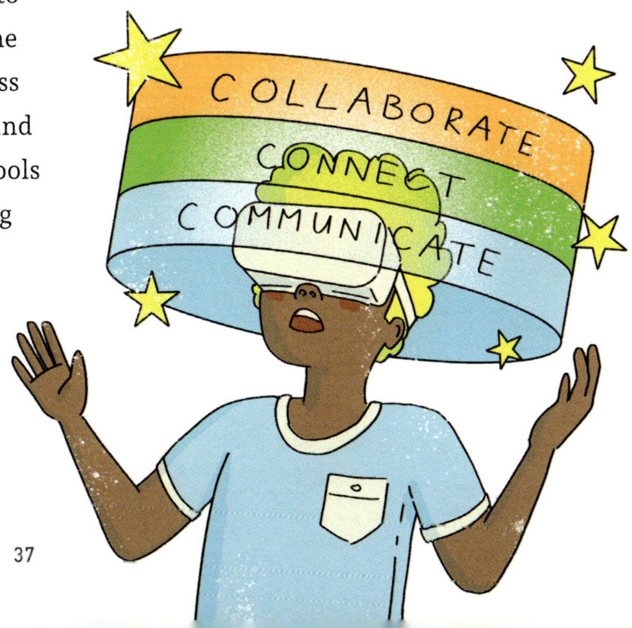

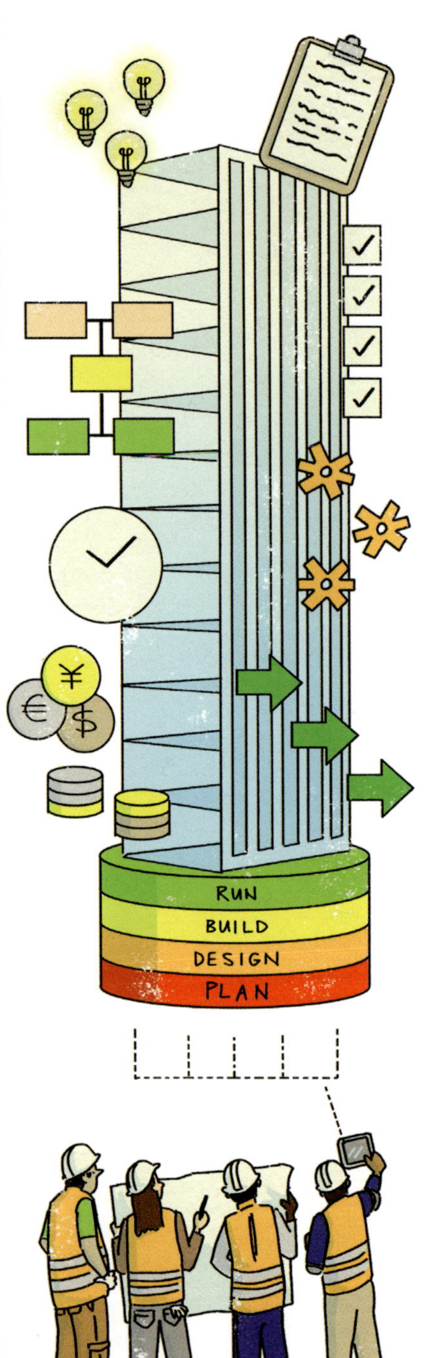

person is in the world. Teams can experience what's being built right from the start. BIM is also connected to a ***database*** of different features, materials and designs. Teams can simulate models and compare them.

BIM, VR, MR, AR, robots, drones and wearables generate and use oodles of data—***big data*** helps us plan, construct and boost safety. The ***Internet of Things (IoT)*** connects smart devices and people so that the big data can be shared. With ***artificial intelligence (AI)***, we can make sense of the data.

Each technology has a job on its own, but together they're super powerful—they provide better communication, connection, transfer of data between devices and people, and problem solving.

Still, we need to use caution when adopting new technology. For example, AI tools are advancing fast—some can even design your dream home. Construction employees worry about hacking or how AI could change or eliminate their jobs. Also, in order to gain the benefits, you need high-quality data. How can employees trust that AI models were trained on good data? As AI becomes popular, its use will require careful regulation and control.

Zoning Mystery Solved

As we learned in chapter 2, old zoning rules are part of the reason that housing is unaffordable. Zoning has prevented the construction of more affordable housing options. But because these laws are so complicated, people don't understand how zoning affects communities. So researchers from almost 60 organizations across the United States formed a team to find a solution. They created the National Zoning Atlas, an online mapping tool with the first-ever digital

When government officials can see how zoning laws block the building of affordable housing, some change the rules. When they don't change the rules, citizens and advocates can use the National Zoning Atlas to prove that governments aren't doing enough.

FRANCESCO SCATENA/ GETTY IMAGES

database of zoning laws. The Atlas uses special software that analyzes, stores and displays map data. Zone in! "For the first time, people can understand our nation's 30,000 plus zoning codes," says Sara Bronin, founder of the Atlas.

Into the Future

From robots and exoskeletons to wearables and digital tools, epic technologies are part of the automation solution. They're helping to build homes better, faster, greener and more safely and cheaply. What's next? Using more innovative technologies to help us reimagine construction and the spaces where we'll live, learn, work and play.

DANGER! DANGER!

Construction workers are suffering. They're in pain, exhausted or worse, dying on the job. Almost 40 percent of deaths are because of falls, slips and trips, according to the United States Bureau of Labor Statistics. Even if the worst doesn't happen, they're getting injured. If workers can't do their jobs safely, everyone suffers. Construction touches all aspects of our lives and boosts our ***economy***. Each new building creates jobs, homes and neighborhood improvements. Injuries cost companies billions of dollars.

FOUR

Home Green Home

Humans have been building shelters with wood since the beginning of civilization. Today science, technology, engineering, arts and mathematics (STEAM) innovations are revolutionizing what we can do with wood. Mass timber (short for massive timber) is one of these innovations for building affordable and sustainable housing. It weighs a fraction of what steel or concrete does but creates superstrong and durable structures. It's also faster and safer to build with and more fire-resistant than traditional wood. Plus, its use can help slow climate change and make people healthier.

Mass timber is the name for a group of engineered (manufactured) wood products made in factories with state-of-the-art technologies. Many layers of small pieces of wood are glued or nailed together to create large, solid, rigid and strong building parts like pillars and panels. The parts can be quickly assembled on the construction site to build homes, schools and other buildings. Look at that! The hottest new thing in sustainable construction is the world's oldest material. Let's take a closer look.

State-of-the-art technologies are used to create mass-timber building parts. In 2025 there were about 38 mass-timber factories in North America.
ELEMENT5

Wood's Changing Story

Wood made an ideal building material for the first ancient temples, modern family homes and small buildings. It was readily available and flexible to build with. But in a fire, wood burns. It rots when wet, and it's too light for tall buildings.

When the Romans invented concrete, it became possible to build grander, durable structures. With the Industrial Revolution, steel and iron became essential materials in construction. Reinforced concrete (steel mixed into the concrete) created a new way to meet the building needs of a growing industrial society.

Today, with an escalating climate crisis, mass timber has become a wood solution for building strong, fire-safe and sustainable structures. There are many mass-timber products, but four are used most often to make floors, roofs, beams, columns and other building sections: cross-laminated timber (CLT), glue-laminated timber (GLT), nail-laminated timber (NLT) and dowel-laminated timber (DLT).

The CARBON LOOP

- Forests ***sequester*** (capture and store) CO_2 from the atmosphere and create the oxygen we breathe.
- Mass timber comes from a variety of trees, mostly Douglas fir, spruce, pine and hemlock.
- When we build with mass timber, carbon stays stored in the wood for the life of the buildings, keeping tons of CO_2 out of the atmosphere.
- When new trees are planted to replace harvested trees, they capture carbon, and the cycle of carbon storage continues.
- When trees die of natural causes or are burned in a fire, they can't absorb carbon anymore. And when these trees decay, they release CO_2. Harvesting trees for mass-timber building salvages wood and prevents the release of CO_2.

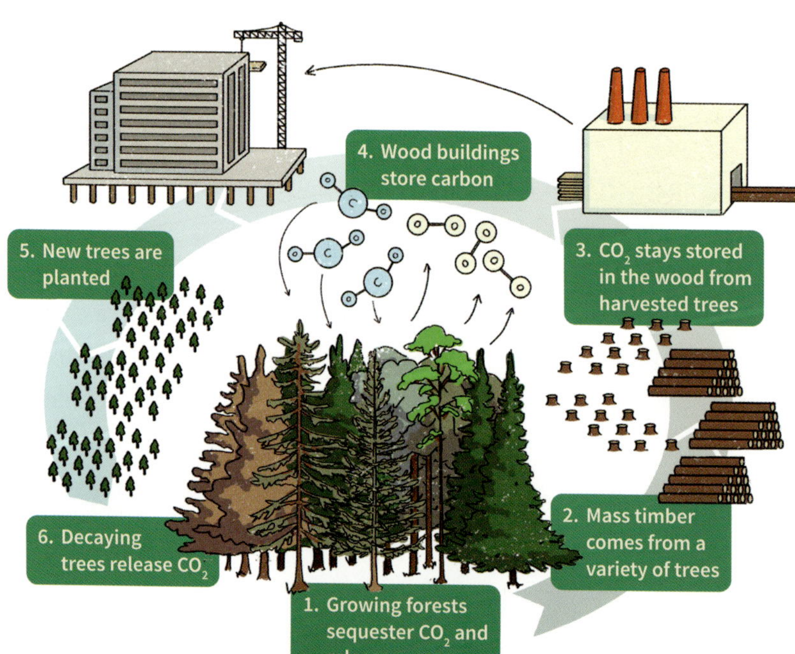

Factory Built

Mass-timber buildings are made like LEGO pieces in a factory (prefabricated or prebuilt) and put together on construction sites. There's a fancy name for this process: design for manufacture and assembly (DfMA). DfMA isn't new—it's already used to produce cars, planes and electronics like smartphones. Now it's being used for housing.

DfMA and mass-timber construction are more sustainable than using concrete and steel. They use less energy, create less waste, reduce CO_2 emissions and make it easier to use recycled materials. They also make construction less expensive, safer and quicker. Plus, the quality is better because machines are accurate to the inch (millimeter). Highly skilled people work in jobs such as 3D modelers or CNC (computer numerical control) operators in DfMA and mass-timber construction.

Patrick Chouinard is the founder of Element5 and a pioneer of mass timber in North America. He says, "Mass timber's bright future will benefit the environment, communities and new generations...we're beginning to build cities out of plant life..."

(MAIN) SOCKAGPHOTO/ SHUTTERSTOCK.COM; (INSET) PATRICK CHOUINARD

Let's Take a Factory Tour!

Element5 is a state-of-the-art, fully automated mass-timber manufacturer in North America. It produces CLT and GLT, which are two of the four types of mass timber. The factory is in St. Thomas, Ontario, where workers use DfMA to design, fabricate and assemble modern mass-timber buildings. Let's step inside!

Wood goes into the factory for processing.

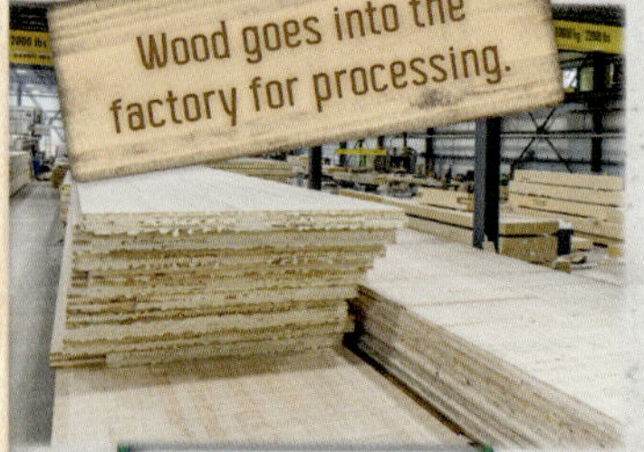

A vacuum lift pulls layers of lumber onto the production line.

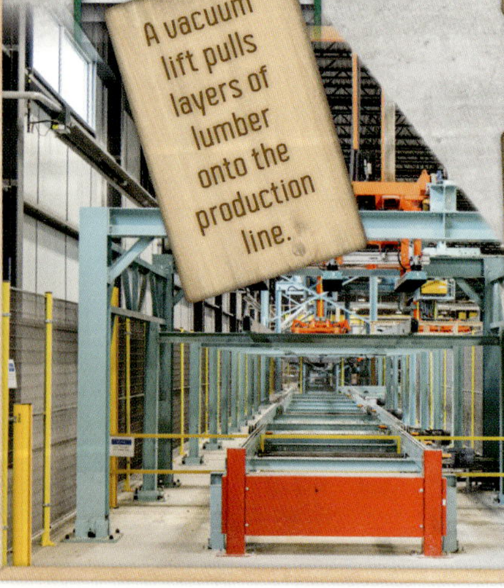

Computer-controlled tools cut and join wood panels using glue, nails, bolts, screws or dowels.

Panels are placed in a press, where tons of pressure squeeze them into strong, layered wood, like thick sandwiches.

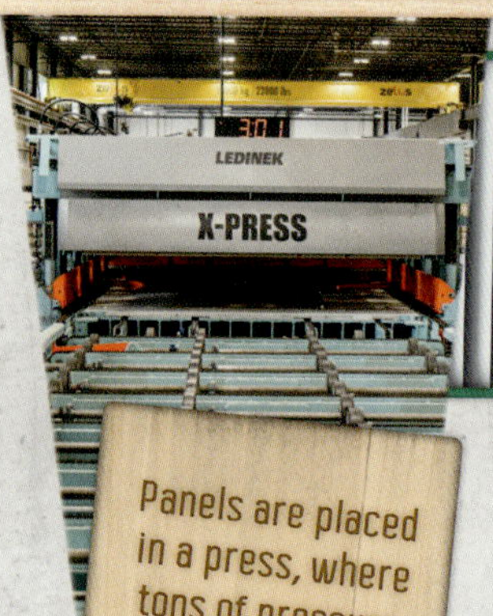

A sander smooths the panels for a clean finish.

CNC machines follow a 3D CAD model to precisely cut, carve, drill or engrave panels, columns or beams.

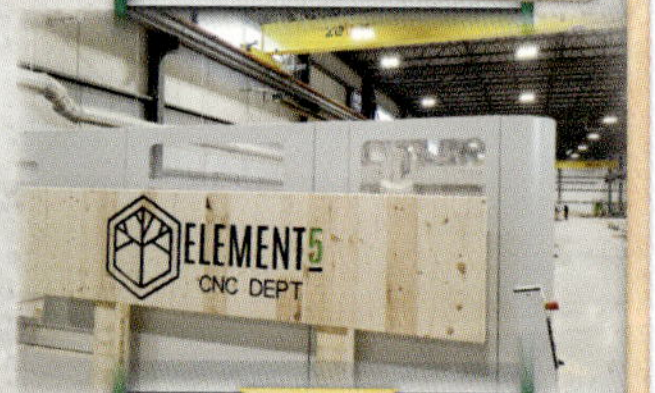

The model details all openings, connections, cuts and grooves, including spaces for windows, doors, mechanical and electrical parts.

The panels, columns and beams are ready for quick assembly at the construction site.

ELEMENT5

Pulling Together: People, Parts and Forces

Mass-timber construction involves skilled experts from many fields. They work together to understand the building as a system—a collection of things that work together. They study the materials that make up the building, and how building parts and services like water and electricity inside work together *and* with the forces outside. They even try to understand how the building makes people feel.

ELEMENT5

MASS-TIMBER MIRACLE

Douglas Cardinal is a well-known Siksika/Métis architect in Canada. Elders from Elsipogtog First Nation in New Brunswick asked him to design better housing for their community. He designed Cardinal House with mass timber made by Element5. It's a ***prototype*** to help meet the housing needs of First Nations peoples who live on reserves. "Conditions are bad," says Elsipogtog First Nation resident Lawrence Dedam. "We don't have enough homes. Families are crammed in one house. Many houses have mold." Homes made from traditional wood don't last in cold, wet, northern climates. Since mass-timber homes are made in factories, they're better made, less expensive and easy to deliver and set up in faraway areas. Cardinal's vision is to create healthy, beautiful homes that last generations.

Green Thumbs-Up

Cutting down trees or salvaging dead ones might not seem like sustainable practices, but they keep forests healthy. Scientists agree that responsible harvesting and salvaging protect the environment and nearby communities.

Fires and insect outbreaks damage trees. When trees decay, they release CO_2. These things are happening more with climate change. And when trees reach old age, their ability to absorb carbon drops. With mass timber, we keep the carbon-capture cycle going by using trees as a building material that continues storing carbon and by regenerating forests with new trees.

There's scientific proof that spending time in nature makes our minds and bodies healthier. We feel happy and less stressed. We also learn and work better. Scientists have a word for our connection with nature: biophilia. It comes from a Greek word that means "a love of living things." Research also shows that when buildings include wood and other natural materials, they can help improve our mental health. Wood buildings feel cozier and warmer than ones made from steel or concrete.

Building with mass timber also helps the economies of communities outside of cities, where many people's jobs depend on the forest industry. And when forest-related businesses do well, it has a domino effect. Other businesses, like stores, movie theaters and hair salons, pop up. It means more jobs and thriving communities for everyone.

Keep the Promise

It's true—Earth's forests are in danger. People have taken away too many trees for agriculture, building, mining,

product manufacturing and other activities. Climate change and endangered species are among the devastating consequences. Illegal logging and other harmful practices destroy forests—full stop. Mass timber is only sustainable *if* people use sustainable forest practices. Wood *must* come from sustainably grown and responsibly managed forests. This means careful planning, strict rules and expert methods.

Let's use Element5 as an example. The company follows Canada's and Ontario's strict rules and laws for tree cutting. "There is virtually zero ***deforestation*** in Ontario," says Patrick Chouinard, the company's founder and former vice president. "That's because only a fraction of one percent of the forest is cut down each year, and forest renewal is required by law. No forest harvesting without renewal! Three trees are planted for every tree that is cut down." Element5 partners only with lumber mills that have international certifications to prove that the wood comes from sustainably grown and responsibly managed forests.

Timber to the Rescue

You might be swimming, working, living or reading in a building made of mass timber. For many years it has been used for community centers, offices, libraries and some of the world's tallest towers. Now it's part of the solution for affordable housing in three important ways. Not only can entire buildings be built quickly, but since mass timber is light, you can even use it to build on top of old buildings. This cool idea makes it easier and faster to add more affordable housing without needing to find new land. In both cases, mass timber is boosting the supply of missing middle housing.

Look—no new land needed! Pathway Non-Profit Community Developments Inc. of Peel and partners used mass timber to add two floors to an existing affordable housing structure in Mississauga, Ontario.

PATHWAY NON-PROFIT COMMUNITY DEVELOPMENTS INC. OF PEEL

TALL TIMBER TALK

Building codes set height limits. The codes vary around the world and change often. Buildings with seven stories or more are called "tall timber" or "tall wood." Most of these are hybrid designs. They combine mass timber with other materials like concrete, steel or both for extra strength and stability. For buildings taller than six stories, wood alone is too light.

The Sky's the Limit

The race is on to see who can build the tallest timber tower! Can these pioneering structures change how we think about wood construction? Can they pave the way for sustainable building design?

Ascent is 25 stories high and 284 feet (86.6 meters) tall—it held a world record in 2022 for the tallest mass-timber hybrid building (it includes steel and concrete). It's in Milwaukee, Wisconsin. Experts say Ascent stores about 7,936 tons (7,200 metric tons) of CO_2.

"Mass timber checks all the boxes," says Tim Gokhman. He led Ascent's development of the first mass-timber tower in the United States. "It's fast, efficient and more precise and sustainable than concrete and steel...I do see this as the future of construction."

SIDEWALKMD/WIKIMEDIA COMMONS/CC BY-SA 4.0

But Ascent won't hold the record for long! An even taller wooden skyscraper is coming to Milwaukee. Michael Green Architecture announced its team's designs for a 55-story tower reaching about 600 feet (182 meters).

In Toronto a team's planning a 31-story hybrid mass-timber tower that's 295 feet (90 meters) tall. In London, England, a team has plans for an 80-story hybrid mass-timber building that is 984 feet (300 meters) tall. And a company in Tokyo is planning a 70-story hybrid mass-timber tower that is a whopping 1,148 feet (350 meters) tall. Whoa!

MODERN MODULAR

Let's learn from history! Prefabricated modular housing isn't a new solution to housing problems. In the early 20th century, DIY "kit" homes were an affordable way to become a homeowner. People picked a design from a catalog, and materials and assembly instructions arrived by train. When soldiers returned home after World War II, countries faced housing shortages, so governments built prefabricated modular housing. Now modular designs made from different materials are back, but with a modern twist, to help today's housing crisis.

New programs are training the next generation of educators, engineers, architects, designers and carpenters in mass-timber construction.

ANDRESR/GETTY IMAGES

Hype or Help?

The global mass-timber movement is on! But are the promises too good to be true?

- Businesses and governments are investing billions of dollars in the mass-timber industry.
- Governments are also updating building codes so that mass-timber buildings can be taller.
- People are learning about mass timber. Some still worry that wood is not strong or that it burns, but rigorous testing proves these things aren't true.

A BALANCING ACT

Sustainable management of forests is essential for both nature and people. Forests support all life on Earth, offering shelter, food, medicine, jobs and income. Sustainable forest management must balance environmental, social and economic needs. Organizations like the Forest Stewardship Council, Sustainable Forestry Initiative and Rainforest Alliance work with governments, businesses and Indigenous communities to set standards that promote ***biodiversity***, protect the ***carbon pool*** and prevent deforestation. They also safeguard workers' rights and local cultures. Only mass-timber products from forests meeting these standards are certified as sustainably and responsibly managed.

Mass timber's future is promising, but there are three key areas people are working to improve:

1. **COST:** Many things affect the price of mass timber. For example, if wood comes from local forests, it will be less expensive than if it comes from far away. A simple building plan will be cheaper than a more luxurious one. If the same plan is used for many buildings, that's another cost saver.

2. **ENVIRONMENTAL FOOTPRINT:** Scientists say we need to know the total carbon story of a building. First, is the wood harvested from sustainably and responsibly managed forests? Second, can experts show that a building will be carbon negative over its lifetime? A lot of things in the construction and operation of a building affect emissions.

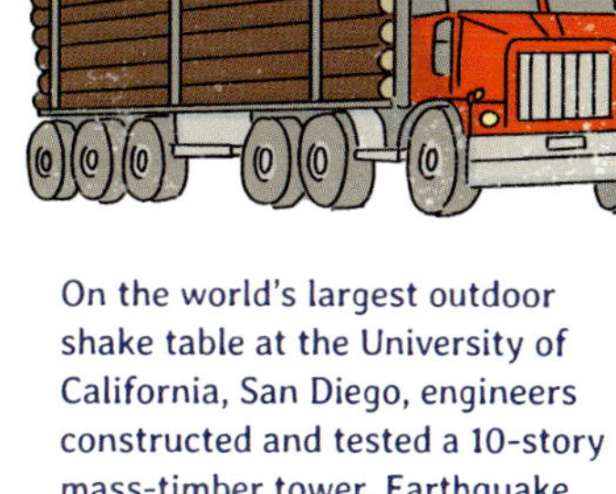

3. **SKILLED WORKFORCE:** Until recently most engineers, architects and skilled tradespeople studied concrete, steel or traditional carpentry. This means there aren't enough people who can make and assemble mass-timber buildings. But this problem will be solved once more programs are offered and as tradespeople with different skills work together.

With each project, experts learn and prove that mass-timber, modular, DfMA construction is a greener, faster and cheaper way to address the housing shortage and the climate crisis. As governments, engineers, architects, builders and businesspeople build alliances and work closer together, we'll see more mass-timber buildings shaping our skylines and sculpting our streets.

On the world's largest outdoor shake table at the University of California, San Diego, engineers constructed and tested a 10-story mass-timber tower. Earthquake test passed! You can watch the live testing on YouTube.

DAVID BAILLOT/UNIVERSITY OF CALIFORNIA SAN DIEGO JACOBS SCHOOL OF ENGINEERING

FIVE

3D-Printed Homes for Hope

Imagine it's an ordinary day and you're walking to school. You turn the corner and see a ginormous 3D printer on a building lot, and it's printing a...house? No, wait...it's printing an entire neighborhood of houses!

It's true. The printer follows a 3D digital model, so there's no limit to the kinds of designs it can create. Then, controlled by robotics and software, it follows a preprogrammed path, squeezing a mixture of materials through a nozzle and depositing it layer by layer until it makes a house. It looks like toothpaste squishing out of a tube!

Trailblazers are climbing a steep learning curve as they learn how to scale up and make neighborhoods of 3D-printed houses that are safe, affordable and sustainable.

SERGII KOLESNIKOV/ GETTY IMAGES

Welcome to the new era of construction. Building-sized printers can now construct a uniquely designed house in days, with only a few workers. But they're hardly just printers—they're sophisticated construction robots! 3D construction printing is advancing fast. Creative thinkers and leaders are pushing the boundaries of what's possible and proving that this technology holds hope for affordable, sustainable housing.

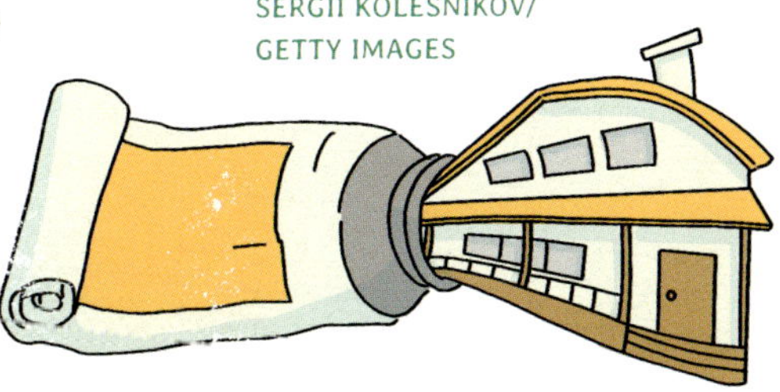

3D printing is fun because it allows you to bring your own creative ideas to life. Imagine it! Design it! Print it!

IZUSEK/GETTY IMAGES

The Rock Star of the Tech World

3D printing sounds futuristic, but it has existed longer than you might think. In 1984 engineer Charles (Chuck) Hull invented the first 3D printer and printing method. This technology captured the imagination of manufacturers and hobbyists alike, and 3D printing grew in popularity. If you can dream it, you can build it.

THERE are THREE MAIN STEPS to 3D PRINTING

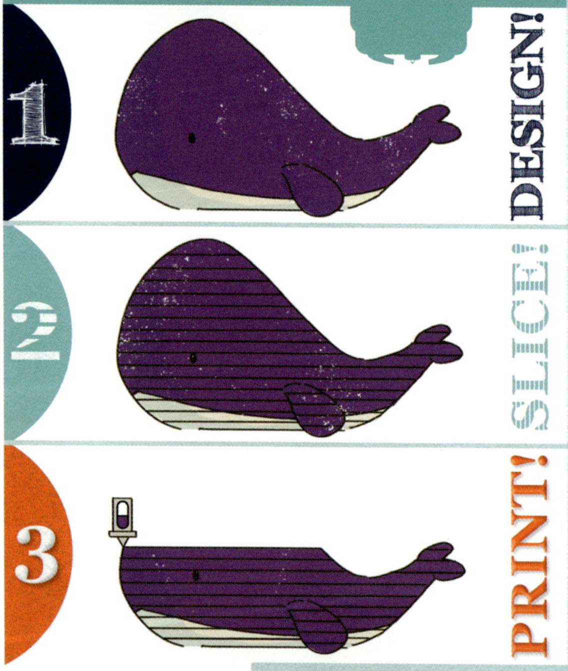

1 DESIGN! Use a computer and CAD software to design a digital model of the thing you want to build. Then save the design in a special file format.

2 SLICE! Each printer has slicing software, which takes the saved 3D design, divides the design into layers and generates instructions to guide the printer on how to create each layer. The instructions are in a programming language called G-code.

3 PRINT! Watch the printer follow a precise path, adding material layer by layer until the object is built. This layering is why it's called additive manufacturing.

Practically any product or part can be 3D-printed, from food, medical instruments and jewelry to robots, prosthetic limbs and even human body parts such as organs and bones. There are many types and sizes of 3D printers. They use different materials, such as plastic, ceramics, glass, metal, biological tissue and concrete.

For many industries, such as aerospace, defense, automotive, robotics and healthcare, 3D printing is a game changer. It's a cheaper, speedier way to manufacture and customize complex products or parts. Since only the exact amount of material is used, there's less waste too.

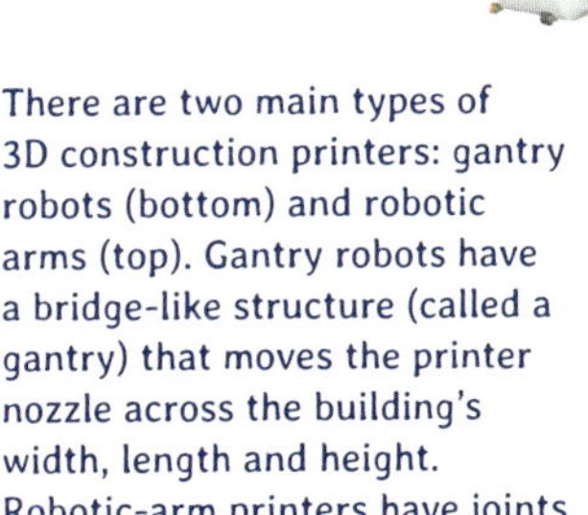

There are two main types of 3D construction printers: gantry robots (bottom) and robotic arms (top). Gantry robots have a bridge-like structure (called a gantry) that moves the printer nozzle across the building's width, length and height. Robotic-arm printers have joints that allow them to move like a human arm and move the printer nozzle in many directions.

ICON

Let's Go Mega-Scale

William E. Urschel invented many machines, and one of them was the world's first wall-building machine. In 1939 he used that machine to create the first 3D-printed concrete building. Other inventors experimented over the years. Then, in 1997, Behrokh Khoshnevis, engineering professor and 3D-printing expert, invented the first modern example of mega-scale 3D printing for construction. He called it contour crafting. This 3D-printing method used a computer-controlled gantry printer, robotics and special materials. Khoshnevis believed that this technology could modernize the construction industry. Seeing homelessness and housing shortages upset Khoshnevis. He also worried about the safety of construction workers. He was on a mission to help with his new technology.

Khoshnevis struggled to get funding to test his new idea. With barely enough money, he experimented by building 3D printers and testing them with different concrete mixes. It was messy and frustrating—the concrete stuck in the nozzle.

Mega-scale 3D construction printing is happening worldwide. People are printing a variety of structures, including houses, offices, bridges and more. Kingston-based nidus3D built Canada's first approved 3D-printed tiny homes and largest 3D-printed housing project, and North America's first 3D-printed multistory building with basement.
NIDUS3D

Finally, in 2004, he got the concrete mix just right. His automated gantry printer system worked!

Khoshnevis's work became famous. Then he started thinking about space. If a 3D printer could work on Earth, why couldn't it work on the moon? On Earth, it prints with cement. But on the moon, it could print with locally sourced lunar regolith (moon dust). Instead of paying millions of dollars to ship materials to space, why not 3D-print shelters on the moon? NASA was excited! In 2014 and 2016, Khoshnevis won prizes from NASA to pay for research to test his idea.

In 2017 Khoshnevis started the first-ever 3D construction printing company. He named it after this new technology—Contour Crafting Corporation. Khoshnevis is continuing his quest to 3D-print affordable housing, and his printer design has inspired many creators.

History in the Making

3D construction printing is advancing quickly. In 2024 there were hundreds of printed buildings worldwide. By the time you're reading this book, there will be *way, way* more. At first only walls could be printed, and buildings had to be small and one story tall. Now buildings can be multistory, and parts like roofs and basements can be printed too.

In 2022 the biggest project ever got underway. A construction technology startup company called ICON and a home-building company called Lennar created the world's first and largest 3D-printed neighborhood. At Wolf Ranch near Austin, Texas, ICON's Vulcan 3D-printing robots printed 100 homes.

Wolf Ranch is a great start, according to Jason Ballard. He's ICON's cofounder and CEO. "But we need to do more—we need a moonshot for housing," he says. Moonshots are projects that use science and technology to develop radically new solutions to huge problems affecting humanity. They're ambitious and risky.

In 2024 Ballard announced a new robotic construction system. It includes a robotic-arm printer called Phoenix that can print multistory structures and many houses side by side. It can also print foundations and roofs. ICON also has a digital catalog of ready-to-print designs and a low-carbon concrete formula called CarbonX.

ICON held a global architecture competition called Initiative 99. Contestants had to design affordable homes that could be built for US$99,000 or less. The homes had to be beautiful, sustainable, comfortable and imaginative. ICON will use some of those designs to build homes for Community First! Village, which helps people in Texas facing homelessness.

The Vulcan gantry printer weighs a whopping 9,500 pounds (4,309 kilograms) and stands 15.5 feet (4.7 meters) tall. It works with the Magma, a mixing unit that prepares ICON's patented material called Lavacrete.

ICON

Phoenix has a high-tech printhead that can position itself, and a crane system to reach different heights. With a few workers monitoring onsite, Phoenix built its first prototype, 27 feet (8 meters) tall and 100 feet (30 meters) long.

ICON

To the Moon and Beyond

If living in 3D-printed structures sounds otherworldly, that's because it is—literally! NASA is planning for long-term human exploration of the moon and Mars under its ***Artemis*** program. It gave ICON special money for their Project Olympus program to research and develop space-based construction systems. ICON will research how to process lunar regolith into a strong building material for 3D printing. Imagine...an entire city made from moon dust and rock, ready for us to inhabit!

At NASA's Johnson Space Center in Houston, Texas, three different crews will take turns living inside a 3D-printed, simulated Martian habitat called Mars Dune Alpha to learn what it's like to live and work on the red planet for long periods of time. Each crew will live there for one year, conducting scientific research. The first CHAPEA (Crew Health and Performance Exploration Analog) crew "returned to Earth" in July 2024, and researchers are studying the crew's health. NASA is planning for its first real mission to the red planet in the 2030s.

Hold on! Don't we have enough housing problems to fix on Earth first before building houses in space? It turns out that the technologies we're developing on Earth will help us build humanity's first home in space. "But it's the other way around too," says Ballard. "Building a human settlement on the moon or Mars will be the most ambitious construction project in human history." It will push science, engineering, technology and architecture to new heights (literally!), and Ballard says that what we're learning will help tackle challenges here on Earth. NASA agrees.

The BOD2 gantry printer weighs 11,883 pounds (5,390 kilograms) and stands 15.5 feet (4.7 meters) tall. It's adjustable for different building sizes, and a team of three to four people can operate the printer.
COBOD INTERNATIONAL/HAVELAR

A Factory on Wheels

A company called COBOD International is also reimagining construction and affordable housing. COBOD stands for "construction of buildings on demand." This company designed a mighty robot printer called the BOD2 (short for "buildings on demand").

Henrik Lund-Nielsen is COBOD's founder and general manager. He says the BOD2 is like a factory on wheels. There are more BOD2 printers in the world than any other 3D construction printers. Projects the BOD2 has built include:

- the first 3D-printed school in Ukraine
- Africa's first 3D-printed affordable homes and schools
- Portugal's first 3D-printed family home
- Canada's first 3D-printed tiny homes and the country's largest 3D-printed housing project
- the first multistory 3D-printed buildings in North America, Europe and India

And there are *way, way* more.

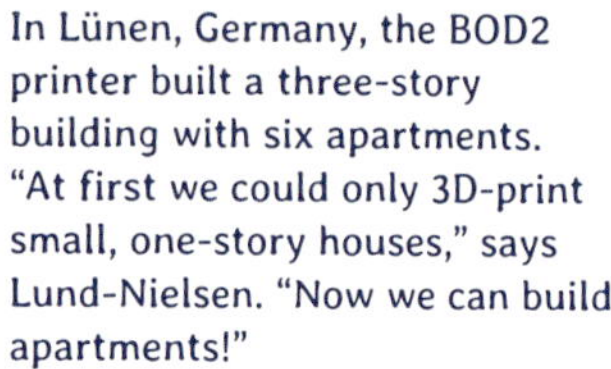

In Lünen, Germany, the BOD2 printer built a three-story building with six apartments. "At first we could only 3D-print small, one-story houses," says Lund-Nielsen. "Now we can build apartments!"

COBOD INTERNATIONAL/
PERI 3D CONSTRUCTION

In 2023 a company called PERI 3D Construction used the BOD2 to 3D-print Europe's first social housing apartment, in Germany. "We can build affordable housing quickly, modernly and sustainably," says Ina Scharrenbach, a government minister in charge of housing for North Rhine–Westphalia. It was the first time a government paid to 3D-print housing. Fabian Meyer-Brötz is the managing director at PERI 3D. "We've proved the technology is ready for widespread use," he says.

In 2024 COBOD announced the BOD3. This mighty machine can build larger buildings and more of them at one time. It's also loaded with advanced robotic features and only needs three people to operate it.

Minister Ina Scharrenbach talks to a PERI 3D worker about how 3D printing is attracting a new generation to construction and offering an exciting solution for creating affordable housing.

COBOD INTERNATIONAL/
PERI 3D CONSTRUCTION

Concrete and Beyond

Concrete is everywhere. It's the most used building material in the world. That's because it's strong and long-lasting. But the key ingredient that gives concrete its strength is cement, and cement manufacturing produces harmful CO_2 emissions.

Researchers worldwide are using science and technology to make low-carbon concrete, whether the material is for traditional building or 3D printing. New methods and formulas are reducing CO_2 emissions. For example, COBOD and ICON invented advanced low-carbon cement to reduce carbon emissions and make 3D printing even more sustainable. But although 3D printers use less material and produce less waste than traditional construction, the global crisis demands more innovation.

So what's next? Experts see enormous possibilities for 3D-printing technology that goes beyond concrete. Exciting projects using locally sourced, natural resources like clay, raw earth, wood fiber and upcycled plastic offer new sustainable solutions.

In 2023, 3DCP and partners used the BOD2 to 3D-print the first low-carbon building in Denmark. It's 775 square feet (72 square meters) and has a gym, guest room and laundry facility for residents of nearby apartment buildings.

COBOD INTERNATIONAL/ 3DCP GROUP

In 2019 WASP built TECLA (short for technology and clay). It's the first eco-habitat made with multiple WASP printers at the same time. Each house is created with entirely reusable, recyclable materials taken from local soil.
WASP SRL

WASP—Like the Insect

World's Advanced Saving Project (WASP) is a pioneering 3D-printing company in Italy. Massimo Moretti is the founder. He wants to build homes that coexist with the environment, not destroy it.

Potter wasps inspired the team. These wasps build nests of mud that are shaped like a vase or jug. Taking its cue from the potter wasp, the company is 3D-printing houses with raw earth, clay and recycled waste materials. They fit with the local climate so they don't need heating or air conditioning, and they blend into natural surroundings.

In 2018 Gaia was the first 3D-printed house in the world to be built with raw earth and waste materials like rice straw and husks. The WASP team built it with their gantry-style 3D printer in just a few weeks.

A Recyclable House?

The BioHome3D is the world's first 3D-printed home made from 100 percent ***bio-based*** materials that are fully recyclable. Each module—the walls, floor and roof—is made from a mix of wood fiber and ***bioplastics***. The home is expected to last for more than 50 years and then all parts can be recycled. It was printed in 2022 at the University of Maine's Advanced Structures and Composites Center (ASCC).

The center worked with the Oak Ridge National Laboratory to learn how to combine wood fiber and bioplastics to make the 3D-printed material. They also figured out how to print the house with almost no waste. Since wood fiber is a renewable resource that captures carbon during the tree growth cycle, the carbon stays stored and protected for the life of BioHome3D.

Frosty Maine winters, hot summers and extreme winds created a challenging building environment. But researchers found that this 600-square-foot (56-square-meter) prototype held up in different conditions. It also meets Maine's rules for building affordable housing.

Time to scale up! Habib Dagher is the executive director of the ASCC. "We've created a house," he says. "Now it's time to create neighborhoods." In 2024 the university unveiled a new printer called the Factory of the Future 1.0. It's part of a new research factory with AI-enabled manufacturing technologies and robotics that opens in 2026 and will train students for the workforce of the future. The goal is to produce new homes faster and cheaper. ASCC is already finalizing plans to print the world's first bio-based 3D-printed neighborhood for people facing homelessness. There will be nine homes in the Greater Bangor region of Maine.

The Factory of the Future 1.0 is a giant robotic manufacturing system. It will print the first neighborhood using bio-based materials. Maine urgently needs affordable houses, but there aren't enough builders. Governor Janet Mills is excited because this technology could help solve the housing crisis.

ADVANCED STRUCTURES & COMPOSITES CENTER AT THE UNIVERSITY OF MAINE

Turning Waste into Homes

Morten Bove is the CEO at WOHN Homes. The Danish company uses clean energy to 3D print tiny affordable homes from upcycled waste plastic and fiberglass (a strong material made from tiny glass threads), and waste wood. Bove wants their homes to tackle climate change and give people equal opportunities for housing.

A tiny home can look good. That's because with 3D printing you have incredible design options. Bove thinks we need to change our view of housing. We need to live smaller, use space better and not think about homes as a sign of prestige. The maximum size of home that WOHN prints is 1,076 square feet

(100 square meters). The average suburban house in the United States is about 2,300 square feet (213 square meters).

Humans produce about 400 million tons (363 million metric tons) of plastic waste every year. Bove says that for each 215-square-foot (20-square-meter) tiny home they build, they take 4 tons (3.6 metric tons) of waste from the environment and save 15 tons (13.6 metric tons) of CO_2. WOHN's building method can reduce the CO_2 footprint by 90 percent compared to building homes with concrete or steel. Bove says the house will last 50 to 60 years. Then the materials can be recycled by adding fresh waste.

WOHN Homes aims to protect biodiversity of the land by keeping the vegetation on site untouched during construction.
WOHN HOMES

Hype or Help?

3D-printed homes are making headlines. Is it all hype because it's new technology? Or can 3D printing really help both the housing and climate crises?

ICON

HELPING THOSE MOST in NEED

Community First! Village in Texas provides homes and services to people facing homelessness. ICON printed a welcome center and a mix of 17 tiny homes and townhomes. More than 100 3D-printed homes are under construction. ICON has also worked with a company called New Story to build 3D-printed homes for struggling families in Mexico. "New technology almost never gets to the people who need it most," says New Story's CEO and cofounder, Brett Hagler.

People are investing billions of dollars. Governments are starting to recognize 3D printing as part of the affordable-housing solution. Some have big plans. For example, the city of Dubai in the United Arab Emirates says that by 2030, 25 percent of the city's buildings will be 3D-printed. Experts say that when big companies and governments invest in new technologies, these are important signals that they're on the right track.

Because of 3D printing, kids in rural Africa have schools, and people who have lost their homes because of poverty, war or natural disasters have somewhere safe to live. And the buildings *are* safe! International organizations are testing, approving and proving that 3D-printed structures stand up to wind, heat, hurricanes, floods, earthquakes, fire and other extreme conditions. The organizations are creating new standards for 3D printing so that governments and building officials can update their building codes.

Maclean's magazine and *SiteNews* each named Ian Arthur as a top influencer and construction trailblazer who's pioneering solutions for the housing crisis.
NIDUS3D

The Next Generation

Ian Arthur is the cofounder of nidus3D in Canada. Arthur's team has used the BOD2 to print the country's first tiny homes, the largest 3D-printed housing structure and North America's first 3D-printed multistory building. Arthur says 3D printing creates exciting, safe jobs, so it's a great way to attract young people to construction. "Our team's incredible," says Arthur. "They come from different trade backgrounds, levels of education and industries."

When Arthur visits middle-grade and high-school students, he asks if they like the idea of working in the trades and working with computers. He tells them that with 3D construction printing, you can do both! When he showed them slides of the BOD2 in action, the students thought it was supercool!

Paige Gaulin worked in a kitchen for 10 years. She says, "Seeing how much food was wasted saddened me. I'm happy we have 3D printers to reduce construction waste."
NIDUS3D

A Steep Learning Curve

Are there challenges with 3D-printing homes? Sure—it's still new technology. There's a skilled-labor shortage. Operating the printer requires special skills, but companies and colleges provide training. Governments are still learning and updating building codes and regulations. And people want proof that 3D printing is cheaper. Experts agree that the costs are coming down as the technology advances and more giant projects like ICON's 100-house community are built.

Companies are continuously improving their printers, making them faster and more efficient. They're also refining the material mixes to ensure they're heavy-duty, eco-friendly, efficient and locally available. 3D printing is advancing construction automation, and new companies are springing up.

Brodie Ladd worked in construction for 15 years. He says, "I feel lucky to work with this amazing new technology and help build homes more efficiently."
NIDUS3D

Nhung Nguyen, CEO of Horizon Legacy, says her team is reimagining construction. "With cutting-edge technology, we're inspiring the next generation to love building. VAL 2.0 handles the backbreaking, repetitive tasks, letting our engineers do the creative work like programming and supervising."

HORIZON LEGACY CONSTRUCTION AUTOMATION

Innovators have a dream, and the guts to take a risk. They're on a steep learning curve, but with each new project, they're improving. A lot of math, science and engineering is behind the development of the materials and equipment. Learning from failures is important.

Stay tuned! Soon 3D printing will move from being headline news to being the typical structures in which we live, learn, work and play. It's not all hype!

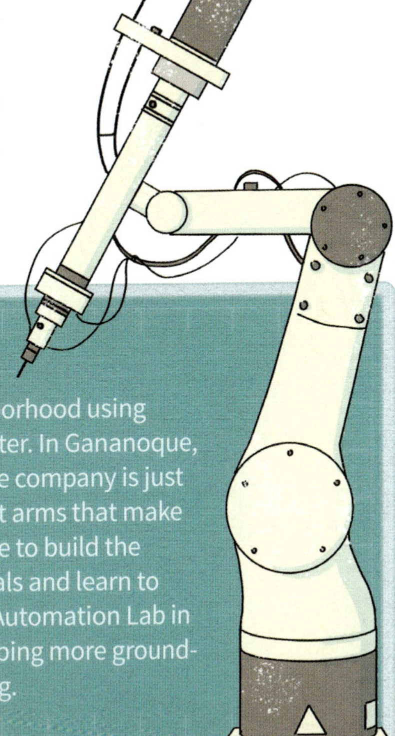

ROBOTICS on the WORKSITE

Horizon Legacy built Canada's first and largest 3D-printed neighborhood using onsite robotics. VAL 2.0 is the company's mobile robotic arm printer. In Gananoque, Ontario, this bot 3D-printed 26 stacked townhouse units—and the company is just getting started! VAL 2.0 was designed to work like the smart robot arms that make cars. With speed and precision, VAL 2.0 deposits layers of concrete to build the walls. In the future the bot will be able to work with other materials and learn to build more parts of the building. At the company's Construction Automation Lab in Toronto (the first one in Canada), they're researching and developing more groundbreaking technology to help build affordable, sustainable housing.

SIX

Creators Unite!

Having a home means something special to each one of us. Home is at the heart of our health, happiness, safety, security and opportunity. Here's how students in the Meaning of Home contest run by Habitat for Humanity Canada describe it:

"Home, a Place of Love and Laughter"

By Harleen

Home is where my family is,
my mom and dad, my brother too,
where love is shared and bonds are strong,
and memories are made with
the ones we love.
...Home is where we celebrate holidays
and special occasions making
traditions and creating memories
that will last a lifetime...

VIJAY SEMPLA

JOHN W. LAM

"MY HOME IS MADE WITH LOVE"

BY JOHN

My house is made with concrete.
My home is made with love.
Love. Peace. Kindness.
...Home is a place that everybody deserves.
Home is a place that should be affordable to all.
To feel safe. To feel free. To dream...

To sustainably meet the needs of our world's soon-to-be 10 billion people, we need to build homes differently. Technology can help. But no single technology or building material will do the job—we need many options. And we need something else—collaboration! Teamwork puts projects on the path to success. Here's a surprising fact: technology can spark collaboration. People have been trying to fix housing problems for decades. Today technology helps people reimagine how to design and construct buildings. But innovating is hard. It takes guts, risks and money. A lot of people are challenging old rules and ideas. They're proving they can do construction differently and, most important, help solve the housing crisis.

Warm and Cozy

In 2021, after years of facing homelessness, 41 women moved into new homes. Their apartment building was the first-ever mass-timber affordable-housing project in Ontario.

The YW Kitchener-Waterloo has been helping women and their families for over 100 years. Like most cities in North America, the Kitchener-Waterloo region struggles with homelessness. Elizabeth Clarke is the former CEO of

“It’s time to rethink how we build affordable housing,” says Element5’s Patrick Chouinard. This mass-timber apartment was built quickly and beautifully, and with support services to help people. Chouinard believes that warm and welcoming places are important for everyone.
ELEMENT5

this YWCA. She says the emergency shelters weren’t helping women. They needed permanent housing with support programs that created a sense of community.

So they gathered experts to come up with a solution. The Government of Canada agreed to pay for the housing project with money from its National Housing Strategy. But there were rules—the houses had to be built within 12 months. The City of Kitchener donated land. Element5 partnered with Edge Architects and a team of engineers, builders, tradespeople, fire experts and others. The Ontario government contributed money to help build Element5’s factory.

“We thought carefully about the best design,” says Matt Bolen from Edge Architects. “Some women were fleeing violent situations or crowded shelters without privacy. We wanted to create a sense of warmth and well-being. The wood is cozy and calming.” One resident says she finally feels safe in her own quiet, beautiful apartment with doors that lock. There’s even a dining room where the residents all eat together.

Creating healthy housing improves people's health and thereby builds healthy communities.
ELEMENTS

TWENTY DAYS!

The core structure for the 41 apartment units went up in 20 days. Within a year the building was finished, and people were living in it. Record speed was possible because of mass-timber technology. Since this way of building was new for some team members, they worked on the design-build project together from the beginning. Bolen says that's not the usual way construction works, but it made things go a lot faster.

This apartment complex was so successful that in 2023 the team built another one in less than one year. This time it was built especially for mothers and children who were experiencing homelessness.

A Model for Others

Let's think differently about how to design healthy communities. Step one—build homes for people in need that have places where they can meet and share their cultures.

The Vancouver, BC, neighborhood around Main and Cordova Streets is in the city's Downtown Eastside. This is a historic part of Vancouver where many people don't have homes and live on the streets. The BC government's Mass Timber Demonstration Program (MTDP) aims to help.

The program is funding 20 buildings and eight research projects to help people worldwide learn about mass timber. The buildings include homes, schools, offices, stores, Indigenous centers and other structures. The hope is that the MTDP will help update building rules, solve housing issues, fight climate change, create jobs and make communities healthier.

A new building at the corner of Main and Cordova will be one of MTDP's first affordable mass-timber apartments and a model for others. When it's done in 2026, it will have

120 units. Residents will also be able to get help with jobs, medical care and support for mental health issues and addictions. But that's not all.

The project team is taking a "living heritage approach." That means honoring peoples' values, skills and ways of knowing to shape communities today and in the future. This neighborhood has a rich mix of Indigenous, Chinese Canadian and Japanese Canadian people whose ideas will guide the building's design. For example, when asked, people said they wanted safe, livable spaces to connect with each other and nature. Each floor will have gathering spaces. There will be a rooftop garden; a courtyard with benches, tables and play areas; shops; a learning center; and a theater space for cultural celebrations. The theater will be a place where residents can celebrate traditions through music, art and storytelling. First Nations' history and learnings along with the other cultural heritages will be important influences on the design.

3D-Printed Homes for Youth

In 2022 four tiny 3D-printed homes in Leamington, Ontario, were the first of their kind in the country. Canada Mortgage and Housing Corporation (CMHC), the government's housing agency, said this trailblazing project set a new standard for affordable housing in the country. It's addressing the housing shortage and modernizing how we think about building communities.

For young homeless people, not just any housing will do, says Krista Rempel, The Bridge's executive director. They need housing with supports, such as someone to talk to, mental health and addiction services, and help with school or job searching.

NIDUS3D

nidus3d is a Canadian leader in 3D construction printing. The company was still running tests on its BOD2 printer when its cofounder, Ian Arthur, got a call. It was from Fiona Coughlin, executive director and CEO at Habitat for Humanity Windsor-Essex in Ontario. She said their local Habitat office had received money from the Government of Canada's housing agency to build affordable housing, but it had to be built fast and with new technology. Arthur agreed. He said his company would speed up testing and then learn as they built.

The University of Windsor is nearby. It has the largest structural engineering lab in Canada. Engineers had been studying and testing 3D construction printing. So their team joined the project. Krista Rempel, executive director of the Bridge Youth Resource Centre, had land and was planning to build a tiny-home community for homeless youth in the city. Rempel came on board. Since building codes in Canada weren't approved for 3D printing, everyone agreed that city planners and building officials from the Town of Leamington would also join the group. They would be the ones to approve the housing, so they had to learn about and trust this new technology.

BUILD, TEST, REPEAT AND CHEER!

The team knew this project would be hard because homes had not been 3D-printed in Canada before. They faced many problems, like getting the material just right for the changing weather conditions, adjusting the printer's position to fit the site and proving that the structure was safe for heavy loads. Coughlin says each house could take the weight of 90 parked cars.

There was a lot of trial and error, but everyone patiently learned together. Friends of The Bridge built a greenhouse for testing insulation. Habitat for Humanity's volunteers helped build parts that were not 3D-printed, such as the roof, windows and doors. And neighbors cheered from the sidelines. "It was the opposite of NIMBY—it was YIMBY!" says Coughlin.

The young people love their new 3D-printed homes. Some have never lived in their own spaces. "They think they're supercool," says Rempel. "It's all about helping youth reach their potential and creating a safe and ***inclusive*** community they can grow into."

Coughlin says that none of the organizations could have done this project alone. Now all eyes are on Leamington. When she presented the project to the Ontario Building Officials Association, they were excited and wanted to learn about 3D printing.

The team proved that 3D printing is an efficient, affordable, sustainable solution for housing Canadian families. Coughlin says that when you're rising to a challenge like the housing crisis, you can't be afraid to try new solutions.

Four beautiful, tiny 3D-printed homes are proof that solutions to the housing crisis are possible.

NIDUS3D

Guiding Stars and Stories

In 2024 the nidus3d team traveled over 2,000 miles (3,379 kilometers) with their BOD2 printer, from Ontario to the Siksika Nation reserve in Alberta, to build Kakatoosoyiists, Canada's largest 3D-printed housing project.

There are four buildings on the site, each with four small apartments. "The homes will help people in our community at risk of becoming homeless," says Ryan Hall, the Siksika Nation's housing manager. *Kakatoosoyiists* is the Siksikáí'powahsin word meaning "Star Lodges." Hall says the name comes from stories about how stars can provide guidance, a sense of direction, protection and life lessons to the people who live in these homes.

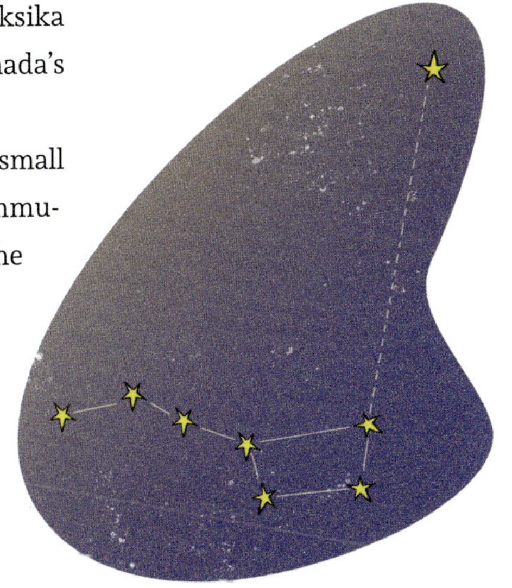

Welcome to the construction site of the future! Built to the latest international standards, Kakatoosoyiists, a massive, strong building, was printed in five days. It will bring hope to people in dire need and advance automation in the construction industry.
NIDUS3D

nidus3D and the University of Calgary School of Architecture designed and built the homes with input from Knowledge Keepers and Siksika Nation members. The concrete company Lafarge provided low-carbon cement, and Indigenous Services Canada gave money. The project also created new training and jobs for Siksika Nation contractors and youth.

Since the Siksika Nation is in a cold and windy area, the team came up with new ways to insulate the buildings to keep them warm. They also created new ways to secure the roof to the building, and they figured out a different delivery system for the concrete mix. All these innovations will advance the future of 3D construction printing.

3D Printing Helps Global Tragedies

When disasters such as war or floods strike, people need to organize quickly. 3D printing is a speedy new way to help with ***humanitarian aid***.

AFFORDABLE GREEN HOMES AND SCHOOLS IN AFRICA

Africa's population is growing, and resources are scarce. There is a desperate need for homes and schools. Two companies, Holcim Group and British International Investment, along with other partners, put their brainpower, money and technologies together to help. They created a charity called 14Trees. "You can solve two problems at once," says François Perrot, the managing director of 14Trees. You can build faster with better quality at a lower cost. This will make affordable housing possible for more people. And by using fewer materials, we're preserving resources for future generations. In 2021, 14Trees built the world's first 3D-printed school in Malawi and in record time. The walls went up in 18 hours.

14Trees also built Africa's largest affordable-housing project, in Kilifi, Kenya. There are 52 eco-friendly homes in a new neighborhood called Mvule Gardens, and more on the way!

This primary school in Mcheza village, Malawi, helps thousands of children. According to UNICEF, Malawi is short of 36,000 classrooms. Building them the usual way would take 70 years, but with 3D printing, they could be built in just 10 years.

14TREES

REBUILDING HOPE IN UKRAINE

In 2022 Russia attacked Ukraine. The war hit the country hard. Families lost their loved ones. Bombs destroyed homes, schools, stores, hospitals and bridges. Jean-Christophe Bonis and Dominique Piotet wanted to help. They are tech leaders at Humanitarian Innovative Technologies (HIT). Together they set up Team4UA. It's a humanitarian foundation that responds to world emergencies with cutting-edge technology.

More than 2,000 schools in Ukraine were damaged, and 330 were demolished. But, layer by layer, Team4UA is rebuilding the country. They partnered with Mikkel Brich's team from the 3DCP Group in Denmark and used the BOD2 to build Europe's first 3D-printed school in Lviv. "Children deserve quality education," says Bonis. "Their future, and the future of the state, depends on it." The 3D-printed school is a model for the reconstruction work that lies ahead.

Jean-Christophe Bonis says, "I have children coming to me with their parents and telling me in Ukrainian, 'I will be in this school, I'm so excited, my school is unique in the country.'"
COBOD INTERNATIONAL/TEAM4UA

Just the Beginning

Trailblazers are proving that we can do construction differently—we can build affordable, green housing and create healthy communities.

- Tall timber towers are lining our skylines.
- Middle-size, affordable mass-timber housing is on the rise.
- Scientists are producing low-carbon concrete and experimenting with organic materials.
- Inventors are making 3D printers with more robotic functions and developing methods to print with raw earth, clay, upcycled plastics, waste materials and wood fibers.
- Immersive technologies and smart design tools are helping people collaborate and reimagine the spaces where we live, learn, work and play.
- Exoskeletons and other wearables are keeping workers safer.
- Robots, drones and other technologies are our superhelpers.

WHAT'S NEXT?

More innovation!

Canadian architect Michael Green builds with mass timber. "We *can* solve this combination of human need and the planet's need at the same time," he says. Wood is good, but it's not the total solution. Green thinks we'll discover what's next for building sustainable homes by studying nature and making organic materials from forests and crops. "We're way past an industrial revolution of materials," he says. "We are at the beginning of Mother Nature's revolution!" He wants to create new carbon-sequestering, plant-based structures and a way to use as little material as possible. High-tech tools like computer modeling and robotics will be key helpers.

The future is also about scaling up from one-off prototypes to building entire neighborhoods and communities. "If we can 3D-print 100 homes, we can do 1,000 and then 10,000," says ICON's Jason Ballard. "We want to build a house per day, then a house per hour, per minute, and then per second! At a house per second, we can solve the global housing crisis in our lifetime!"

The possibilities are astounding. But experts agree that *total* automation is not the answer or the goal. Beautiful, eco-friendly homes that help *everyone* live with dignity—that's the goal.

Creative brains are needed! When people work together and use technology, powerful changes are possible. We *can* fix the biggest forces affecting people's health and well-being. But we'll need to take risks and innovate and keep proving to the world that construction can be done differently.

In 2022 Peris+Toral Architects built Spain's largest social-housing apartment complex, called Terraces for Life. It has 40 apartments with open living spaces, and a rooftop greenhouse connects residents with nature.

TERRACES FOR LIFE BUILDING BY URBANITREE, DANIEL IBAÑEZ AND VICENTE GUALLART

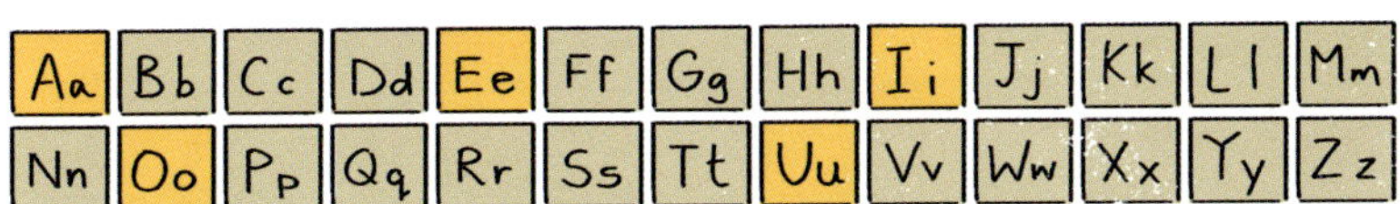

Get Innovating!

How do you imagine our homes of the future? Are you ready to get innovating?

GET STEAMING

- Go to a nearby school, a library makerspace or a camp to learn 3D printing.
- Imagine your dream home. You can create a design in CAD and 3D-print it.
- 3D-print a robot or drone and enter your design in an engineering challenge. Or check out Poppy Project, a community-centered robotic project. Anyone can join for free and build a Poppy robot.
- Materials science is at the cutting edge of science and engineering. Can you turn milk into plastic? Maybe one day you'll invent a biomaterial for 3D-printing houses!

What will you create? 3D printing pens are fun tools to get you started learning about 3D objects.

MARINA DEMIDIUK/GETTY IMAGES

Get Building

- Ask your teacher if your class can build a tiny home. That's what eighth-grade woodshop students at Nicholas Junior High in Fullerton, California, did.
- Volunteer with Habitat for Humanity or another organization to help build tiny homes.

Get Writing

Write a poem, story or essay. Here are some ideas to get you started.

- What does having a home mean to you?
- Why do you think housing is a human right?
- How do you think 3D printing or mass timber could address a housing need in your community?
- What do you think are the pros and cons of 3D printing for home building?
- What do you think are the pros and cons of mass timber for home building?
- Build a word cloud to capture how tech innovation is shaping the future of housing construction.

GET FUNDRAISING

- Do some research about projects in your area that help people build safe places to live. How can you help?

GET CAREERING

- Modern construction uses smart, green technology. Flip back through this book and think about which jobs and technologies you'd like to know more about. Ask your teacher to invite an expert to your classroom to talk about their jobs and the technologies they use to build homes.

Want a high-flying career? The job of a drone pilot is "taking off." Drone use is soaring worldwide. Industries need people to build, program and fly drones. Colleges offer programs and certificates to teach students how to fly drones safely.

DMITRY KALINOVSKY/SHUTTERSTOCK.COM

GLOSSARY

actuators—the parts of devices that convert energy into physical motion. The motion can be along a straight line (linear) or spinning around from a center point (rotational). There are many types of actuators. The three most common ones are hydraulic, pneumatic and electric. In robotics, the actuator enables a robot to move.

Artemis—name of NASA missions to explore the moon for scientific discovery and technology advancement

artificial intelligence (AI)—a technology that focuses on creating machines that can simulate human intelligence. Machine learning that can match or exceed the abilities of a human in performing a task is called strong AI, or artificial general intelligence.

automation—automatically controlled operation of a device, process or system by devices instead of people

autonomous—capable of performing a task with little or no human assistance

big data—massive amounts of data from different sources that are speedily created, analyzed and then processed over the internet

bio-based—products or materials that come from plants and other renewable agricultural, marine and forestry materials

biodiversity—the variety of all living things and their interactions

bioplastics—plastics made from plant-based renewable and biodegradable sources like corn and sugarcane. Bioplastics, also known as bio-resins, are considered the future of sustainable materials.

carbon dioxide (CO_2)—the gas formed when organic matter decomposes, when people and animals breathe out and when carbon is burned. It is a greenhouse gas and a main driver of global climate change.

carbon pool—a place that takes in or releases carbon. There are four carbon pools on Earth: the Earth's crust, the ocean, terrestrial ecosystems and the atmosphere. Forests, pastures, wetlands and croplands are the major terrestrial carbon pools. Forests are the largest above-ground pool of carbon, with carbon stored in the trees, plants and soil.

cloud—the global network of servers, accessed over the internet, that store and deliver data. When something is in the cloud, it's stored on internet servers instead of your computer's hard drive.

computer-aided design (CAD)—the use of computer software to digitally create 2D drawings and 3D models of real-world products before they're manufactured

data—in computer science, basic facts and figures a computer uses to perform tasks or make decisions. Text, emails, apps, pictures, audio clips and other data are processed and stored in numeric code (binary digits with a value of one or zero).

database—a collection of data that is specially organized so people can search and find information quickly

deforestation—removal of trees by humans

economy—the system of how money is made and used in a country or region. It involves how many goods and services are produced and how much people spend on them.

GPS—global positioning system, a space-based satellite navigation system that provides time and location information

homelessness—the state of being without a permanent, appropriate place to live

housing market—the supply and demand for residential properties, including houses and apartments, in a given area. It's influenced by such factors as the supply of housing being built, the number of people who want to buy and sell houses and what they can afford, the growth of the economy and what government is doing to affect housing prices.

humanitarian aid—immediate short-term help to relieve suffering during emergency situations

inclusive—open to everyone, regardless of race, gender, sexuality or ability

Internet of Things (IoT)—the world's collection of smart, connected things (devices, machines, sensors) that generate big data

lidar—a method for determining the distance to an object by transmitting a laser beam (powerful focused light) at the object and measuring how long it takes the light to return to the transmitter. The term is short for *li**ght** **d**etection **a**nd **r**anging*.

machine learning algorithms—a set of mathematical steps or rules that enable machines to learn from data, recognize patterns, make decisions and perform a specific task better over time, becoming "smarter"

policies—sets of rules, laws or plans that guide decisions and actions

prototype—a test model or early version of a product or technology

radar—a system that uses waves of energy to sense objects. It can find a faraway object and determine how fast it's moving. It can detect objects even at night and through thick clouds.

sensors—devices that detect and measure physical properties (such as temperature, sound, pressure or movement) in surrounding environments and convert them to a signal that can be read by an instrument or observer

sequester—capture and store carbon dioxide from the atmosphere

stereotypes—commonly held ideas about certain people or things that are based on prejudices, uncritical thinking, oversimplified opinions or how those people or things look on the outside

stigmatize—to describe or treat someone or something in a strongly disapproving way

sustainable—refers to a way of using natural resources that doesn't deplete or permanently damage them, thereby preserving them for future generations

upcycle—create a new product with a new function from something that's no longer in use

wearable devices—technologies that are on, in or attached to our bodies

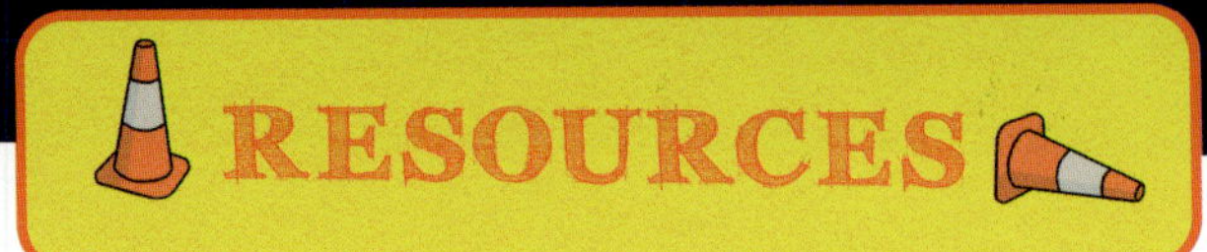

PRINT

Craigie, Gregor. *Why Humans Build Up*. Orca Book Publishers, 2022.

Dyer, Hadley. *More Than Money: How Economic Inequality Affects EVERYTHING*. Annick Press, 2022.

Forde, Cindy. *Bright New World: Building a Better Planet*. Welbeck Children's Books, 2022.

Huddleston, Emma. *Become a Drone Pilot*. BrightPoint Press, 2021.

Peterson, Lois. *Shelter: Homelessness in Our Community*. Orca Book Publishers, 2021.

Mason, Paul. *Building the World: Engineering*. Rosen Publishing Group, 2024.

McMillan, Kate. *Sustainable Structures: 15 Eco-Conscious Buildings Around the World*. Holiday House, 2024.

Orr, Tamra B. *Working with Tech in Construction*. Rosen Publishing Group, 2021.

Scientific American Editors. *Design & Build It: 10 Fun Engineering Projects*. Scientific American Educational Publishing, 2022.

Voss, Elizabeth Hobbs. *Become A Construction Building Inspector*. BrightPoint Press, 2023.

Ziefert, Harriet. *Be Thankful for Trees: A Tribute to the Many & Surprising Ways Trees Relate to Our Lives*. Red Comet Press, 2022.

ONLINE

Websites

Archintect: archinect.com

BC Council of Forest Industries, *Forest Education:* cofi.org/forest-education/fun-activities-resources

FIRST: firstinspires.org/robotics/frc

FIRST Canada: firstroboticscanada.org

Habitat for Humanity: habitat.org

Honour the Work: honourthework.ca

Let's Talk Science: letstalkscience.ca

Meaning of Home Contest: meaningofhome.ca

Poppy Project: poppy-project.org/en

Project Learning Tree: plt.org

Royal Architectural Institute of Canada: raic.org/architecture-schools

Science Buddies: sciencebuddies.org

SolidWorks: solidworks.com

The Skyscraper Museum: skyscraper.org/school-and-camp-visits

Tinkercad by Autodesk: tinkercad.com

United States Department of Agriculture, Forest Service: Discover the Forest: discovertheforest.org

University of Maine, BioHome3D tour: composites.umaine.edu/advanced-manufacturing/biohome3d

Videos

Could We Build a Wooden Skyscraper? TedEd YouTube Channel.

The Material That Could Change the World...for a Third Time. TedEd YouTube Channel

What Happens If You Cut Down All a City's Trees? TedEd YouTube Channel

Links to external resources are for personal and/or educational use only and are provided in good faith without any express or implied warranty. There is no guarantee given as to the accuracy or currency of any individual item. The author and publisher provide links as a service to readers. This does not imply any endorsement by the author or publisher of any of the content accessed through these links.

DEAR READER

Imagine working on a school project where the facts kept changing because the topic was so new—that's what happened while I was writing this book. It was exciting to see progress toward solving housing problems, but also my biggest challenge. I work hard to make sure young readers get accurate nonfiction, so if you spot an outdated fact, that's because more exciting changes are happening. Thank you for caring about housing and the environment.

ACKNOWLEDGMENTS

My deepest thanks to the brilliant team at Orca Book Publishers for helping bring this book to life. First and foremost, I'm so grateful to my editor, Kirstie Hudson, who asked insightful questions and helped me organize my thoughts. To illustrator extraordinaire Catherine Chan and talented designer Troy Cunningham, thank you for making this book so beautiful. My thanks also to Georgia Bradburne for editorial assistance.

To all the innovators who appear throughout this book, it's an honor to feature your hard work and dedication to solving both the housing and climate crises. Your innovative solutions have not only been featured but also deeply respected and instructive.

This book would not have been possible without the contributions of many people. Ian Arthur (nidus3d), Claire Belerique (Horizon Legacy), Josh Caputo (Humotech), Patrick Chouinard (Element5), Fiona Coughlin (Habitat for Humanity Windsor-Essex), Paige Gaulin (nidus3d), Brodie Ladd (nidus3d), Krista Rempel (The Bridge), Roman Spektor (Pathway Non-Profit Community Developments) and Karl Zelik (HeroWear), thank you for answering all my questions and sharing your incredible stories and photos.

The opportunity to watch 3D construction printing happen live and witness cutting-edge moments in housing-construction history was truly remarkable. I'm especially grateful to Ian Arthur and team (nidus3D), Nhung Nguyen and Daniel Cantor (Horizon Legacy) and team, Morten Bove and Matúš Uríček (WOHN Homes), Mikkel Brich and Hasan Alsofi (3DCP Group), and to Krista Rempel and Fiona Coughlin for the chance to visit the 3D-printed homes at The Bridge. To Habib Dagher and Jacob Ward at the University of Maine's Advanced Structures and Composites Center (ASCC), I'd like to express my sincere thanks for the chance to tour the BioHome3D and see the Factory of the Future 1.0 printer.

Many thanks to Robin Wakelin (Habitat for Humanity Canada). I truly appreciate your excitement for this book and making it possible for me to feature the incredible poems of Daphne, Harleen, John, Peyton and Rylan. Kids, your reflections on the meaning of home are nothing short of awe-inspiring.

To Jarett Gross (Automate Construction), I've learned so much from your podcasts and YouTube channel—thank you for sharing your learning.

Many experts kindly agreed to read and provide feedback on the manuscript. My sincere thanks to everyone for your time, thoughtful suggestions and enthusiasm for this book: Ian Arthur, Daniel Cantor, Josh Caputo, Patrick Chouinard, Fiona Coughlin, Georgiabelle (Young Editors Project), Jarett Gross, Habitat for Humanity Canada Communications Team, Nhung Nguyen, Krista Rempel, Karl Zelik and, at the University of Maine's ASCC, Wesley Bisson, Andrew Foster, Amber Hubbard and Halil Tekinalp. As always, my family has been a constant source of support, love and encouragement. I want to express my deepest thanks to my husband, Michael, and daughters, Nicole and Allison.

INDEX

Page numbers in **bold** *indicate an image caption.*

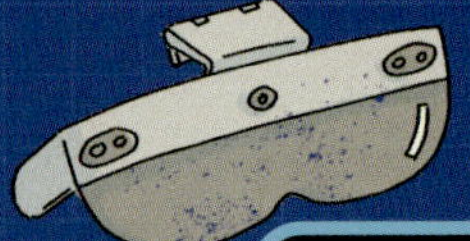

DOROTHY PUDDESTER

ELAINE KACHALA is the award-winning author of *Superpower? The Wearable-Tech Revolution*. With over 20 years as a health-policy writer and adviser, degrees in psychology and sociology (University of Toronto) and a master's degree in environmental studies (York University), Elaine brings a unique perspective to STEAM topics. She hopes to write books that inspire young readers to embrace their curiosity and creativity as they learn about real-life inventors who are unafraid to dream big while thinking critically about health, social and ethical issues. Elaine was also a volunteer therapy-dog handler with her sweet boy, Tucker. Once, when they visited a youth shelter, the kids said that Tucker made their place feel like a home. On personal and professional levels, Elaine is passionate about housing for the health and well-being it brings. She lives with her family in Toronto.

TONY YIU

CATHERINE CHAN is a Toronto-based illustrator with a previous life in project management and technology. Her work explores her relationships as an immigrant, a mother and a lifelong learner, and acts as both self-exploration and self-declaration. She is excited about telling unique and inspiring stories through her illustrations.